Jehovah's Witnesses

Jehovah's Witnesses

Watch Out for the Watchtower!

Gordon E. Duggar

BAKER BOOK HOUSE
Grand Rapids, Michigan 49506

Reprinted 1985, 1987 by
Baker Book House
with permission of the copyright owner

ISBN: 0-8010-2955-4

Printed in the United States of America

To my wife

I watched her tearful, painful struggle as she came free from the bondage of the *Watchtower*. The gnarled mistruths she had grown up in hung to her tenaciously. When she came to know the risen Christ personally, the error fell away like old clothes, layer by layer. Those who know her well know the old and new Vera. Only Jesus Christ can effect such a change—not the *Watchtower* or any organization.

For Jehovah's Witnesses, the "organization" is the ark of safety. No one may reach the Father except through the society. For them there is no truth outside the society. If one is "in the truth," that one is in the organization. If one is outside the organization, one also is outside the only truth.

A JEHOVAH'S WITNESS'S PRAYER

Jehovah, thank you for another day of life. Thank you for our persecuted brothers and sisters throughout the world. Thank you for the physical food we receive and the spiritual food we receive through your organization.

We need to examine, not only what we personally believe, but also what is taught by any religious organization with which we may be associated. Are its teachings in full harmony with God's Word or are they based on the traditions of men? If we are lovers of the truth, there is nothing to fear from such examination.*

*"The Truth That Leads To Eternal Life," The Watchtower Bible and Tract Society, p. 13.

Contents

Preface

I grew up in a small southern town, and my family attended a Baptist church. From my exposure I knew very little about various denominations and religious groups. At the age of eighteen, I moved to a large city to attend college, and as I went back home less and less, I attended church less and less.

Soon I met the girl I later would marry. She told me she was a Jehovah's Witness, which did not seem to make a significant impression on me at the time. Eventually, at her invitation, I went to meetings with her. Her mother and some of her sisters also attended, and her brother-in-law was the leader of the very small congregation. We were married during our four college years. If I was home visiting my parents I went to church; other times (most of the time) I went to the Kingdom Hall. I attended the training sessions for ministers, gave "talks," and went door to door with them. They certainly seemed devoted, so I reasoned there must be something to this.

As more years passed, we moved to a northern city while I continued my education. During this time we stopped attending any services almost entirely. Some years later, after moving back home and after our two older daughters were grown, my wife and I began to feel the need for something more in our lives. We watched preachers on television and went to the Kingdom Hall on Sundays.

Something began to happen to me. I found that I got very irritable when we were at the meetings, and I had increasing difficulty accepting the materials taught there by the "brothers." This restlessness grew until on one Sunday I could hardly resist screaming out at the speaker. On the way home that day I told my wife of my reactions and stated that I would not go back again. My wife, still a strong Witness at that time, neither appreciated nor understood my problem. She felt I would get over this promptly by simply attending services in other churches. We both began to do this; we also began to search. The Witness movement was impressive. I knew these people were very dedicated, sincere, and worked hard at what they believed. But then I realized that I knew very little about the movement itself. I always had difficulty in accepting them as God's *only* organization—*was I wrong?* Obviously, it was important to seek the truth—and peace. So in 1975 I began to research the history of the Jehovah's Witnesses.

I now believe that God has allowed all this for a definite purpose. I did not plan to write a book, but a book came. God has used this experience to liberate me, my wife, and my children. My prayer is that this experience also may be used in the lives of others. There are those in the Witness movement whom I love very much. I hope this book will open their eyes and the eyes of others who are willing to see. May God grant.

Acknowledgments

At a most critical point in our lives along came Aubert Rose, who provided exactly the love and guidance we needed. We also are forever indebted to the impact on our lives of the spiritual teachings of our pastor, Charles Stanley; and to the sweet, praying, supportive fellowship at First Baptist; and especially to Don and Maxine; Ralph and Alice; Walker and Nancy; and Phil and Hazel.

Introduction

A five-year-old child lies seriously ill in the intensive care unit of a large hospital. The parents are anxious and the doctor is very concerned for the life of the child. Because of the severity of the disease, the child is gravely ill and extremely weak. The white blood count and red blood count are dangerously low. Blood is leaving the vessels due to vasculitis and permeating body cavities. The kidneys almost are not functioning. There are many medical problems. As the hemoglobin drops down to below five, the doctor knows that a transfusion can be of immense help. But the parents are Jehovah's Witnesses and have already told the doctor that he may administer any other treatment, but their religious beliefs forbid blood transfusions.

This illustration demonstrates a major doctrine of the Jehovah's Witnesses. They valiantly withhold consent for the use of blood because a man has told them that God forbids this. This is based on certain of the old Jewish laws regarding the eating of animals. Now, their personal investigation of the matter includes only obedience to the admonition they have been given by their leaders. Yet, they are willing to stake the life of their child or even their own life on this obedience. One must not violate a rule of the organization. For a religion that bases many of its tenets on reason, it evidently reasons that God would have some of his own die rather than receive a blood transfusion. It is most interesting that the earliest Jehovah's Witnesses were not subject to this restriction forbidding transfusion, because this prohibition was not enacted until the 1940s. In fact, some earlier Witnesses did have blood transfusions. This is more interesting when we consider that blood transfusions began in the early

1900s, but the Witnesses did not institute this restriction until 1945.

It is interesting to note that in a 1978 *Watchtower,* Witnesses were told they could follow their own conscience in regard to receiving a small amount of blood, such as that found in an injection of serum. Scriptural support for this was not given. This is called a "gray area." Is it gray because Jehovah did not make it clear, or because of a confused *Watchtower*?

Author's Note

It is most doubtful that even Jehovah's Witnesses themselves know the history of their organization. Their early publications are not available to them from The Watchtower Society, and their history is published in changing biased stories. For instance, in a recent *Watchtower* magazine, their "history" was repeated regarding the year 1914 and their prophetic error of that date. They printed simply, "Not all happened that was expected to happen," and they indicated that some small errors were made. One of those small errors was that the world would end that year! So with this type of journalistic dishonesty, one could not expect the straight truth to come forth. Dedicated Jehovah's Witnesses accept anything headquarters tells them—changes and all. They have been instructed that the changes are "new light," and most of them won't ever investigate what is said or is written. They are forbidden to read any material of a religious nature unless they themselves publish it. But we want any Witness reader of this book to know that the material in this book is trustworthy. It is neither altered nor colored. It is a ringside look at the Witness organization through their own literature. This is a true description of the Witness movement with extensive documentation included so that the sources may be confirmed.

I

Jehovah's Witnesses

The religious group known since 1931 as Jehovah's Witnesses follows an organization called the Watchtower Bible and Tract Society in Brooklyn, New York. Until recent years, the Witnesses were considered a radical cult. They became notorious by making repeated sensational predictions and prophecies about such things as the return of Christ and the end of the world. They upheld this notoriety by their refusal to salute the flag, their stand on blood transfusions, their famous court trials, their colorful leaders and their relentless attacks on religion, economics, education and politics.

Now in their hundredth year, they hardly cause a ripple, and most people know little about the reported two million Witnesses. They haven't made any predictions since 1975, and their attacks on others have been markedly reduced to low key. Today they are almost—no, they *seem* almost—like just another Protestant denomination. Some evidence indicates their membership is beginning to decline after having once been called for a short time the world's fastest-growing religion. The fiery leadership of Russell and Rutherford is gone, and the brash organization they led has changed to a much more subtle movement. What has evolved is perhaps the master cult. Theirs is a superstory of mind control.

The early history of the Jehovah's Witnesses begins with the story of two men—"Pastor" Russell and "Judge" Rutherford. Russell "planted" and Rutherford "watered." The crop they produced provides a fascinating study of a new religion, one that feels it is God's only organization. It also tells of a people so totally

1

devoted to this organization that they accept without question all that is sent to them by their leaders. These are people who withheld vaccination of their children (even had them scratched in pretense) until a doubting officer at their headquarters proved that no blood was involved, and who, since 1945, have refused blood transfusions even unto death. Their founder told followers that Jesus would return at a specific date, and they got ready for his coming. After Christ didn't come, Russell told them that Jesus, or his "presence," really did come invisibly or symbolically. So they believed this. They were told that Christ reestablished the nation of Israel and they believed that. Such has continued through these hundred years.

In 1975, the Witnesses expected the world to end, so some sold their belongings, quit their jobs and did similar things since they wouldn't need these activities any longer. It is simply astounding that these followers are so gullible. In regard to the failure of the prophecy of 1914, their literature states simply, "All that was expected to happen didn't occur." And that is good enough for the flock. Initially one man, Charles T. Russell, was the entire mind and spokesman for the organization. After he died, Judge Rutherford succeeded Russell and he also led dictatorily. Rutherford really established the base for the movement, at first continuing Russell's theology but eventually establishing his own theology by writing numerous books. His successor, Nathan H. Knorr, began to show less attention to the individual. Whereas Russell and Rutherford proudly claimed the authorship of their books, this practice stopped with Knorr. The new world society may very well be the master cult.

The mind control tactics used on the followers exposes the deliberate plan used for such control. How does this happen? Witnesses come from all walks of life. They are educated and uneducated, rich and poor, foreign, although originally American. They are instructed not to read religious materials published by anyone other than their society and they don't. Witnesses exhibit an incredibly fierce loyalty to their organization and feel personally offended when the society is attacked. Witnesses are smug, confident. Their literature tells the people whom they are trying to convert to look into their religious beliefs. One book is called *Make Sure of All Things*. Yet, it would be unheard of for a Witness to question his own doctrine. It is simply correct. "I will rise or fall with the organization."

Is this cultism in its purest form? How do these people voluntarily surrender their will and mind and never question whether they are right or wrong? This book is a ringside look at the Jehovah's Witnesses. For thirty years the author was inside, outside and near the organization. Although it will be vehemently denied by the Watchtower Society, this story is true. The facts are not distorted. Unfortunately, most readers will not be Jehovah's Witnesses. They are afraid to read material condemned by their leaders. Their fear of the organization will come out in such activities. The hope of this book is to expose this cunning organization, which makes these people believe that it is God's own—and only—organization. It is also hoped that this book will be a warning. Watch out for the *Watchtower*!

2

The Organization

The religious organization presently called the Jehovah's Witnesses was founded in the United States about the year 1870. Although their literature claims connection back to the biblical times of our early fathers, the truth is that the movement started as another rebellion against conventional Christianity in the mind of a young man named Charles Taze Russell.

Russell was born of Presbyterian parents on February 16, 1852, in Allegheny, Pennsylvania. When he was only a lad, Charles was working with his father successfully operating some clothing stores. Young Russell moved over to the Congregational Church, but he also was troubled by their doctrine, and at the age of seventeen he became by his own admission a "skeptic." He came upon a group called Second Adventists and this "served to reestablish his faith."

Russell began to read the writings of a lady named White. Her writings on death and hell were intriguing to him, and he believed much of her teaching. He became intensely interested in Bible study and in 1870 organized a Bible class of six members, who met for the following four years.

Russell's early writings expressed a belief that Jesus would physically return to the earth and that 1914 would bring the end (not the beginning of the end as later taught) of the world. Russell became acquainted with N. H. Barbour of Rochester, New York. Barbour led a splinter Adventist group that believed that Christ's return would be spiritual rather than physical. Someone in Barbour's group had discovered that the Greek word

4

"parousia," which is rendered as "coming" in the Bible, also meant "present." So with this information, Russell adopted the idea and began to teach with vigor about Christ's second "presence." The two groups, Russell's and Barbour's, joined. Russell supplied the finances, and the magazine entitled *Herald of the Morning* was published. Barbour and Russell also jointly published a book in 1877 entitled *Three Worlds or Plan of Redemption*. The book stated that Christ's second presence began in the fall of 1874.

Soon Russell and Barbour developed irreconcilable differences and they parted. On July 1, 1879, Russell published the first issue of a magazine called *Zion's Watchtower and Herald of Christ's Presence*. Russell's organization began to grow. By 1880, there were small congregations in several states. Zion's Watchtower Society was granted a legal charter on December 13, 1884, and the official name was changed to Watchtower Bible and Tract Society of Pennsylvania in 1896. The purpose of the society as stated in Article 2 of the charter includes ". . . and to prepare, support, maintain and send out to various parts of the world Christian missionaries, teachers and instructors in the Bible and Bible literature and for public Christian worship of Almighty God and Christ Jesus." This statement from their charter will appear again in this book in a section showing the dishonest journalism employed by the society.

In 1886, Russell released the first volume of a series of books that received widespread distribution. Much of the material could be considered sensational religious literature. The first of the seven volumes was called *The Divine Plan of the Ages* and the series first entitled *Millennial Dawn* (referring to, one supposes, the dawn of the millennium of Christ); then the name changed to *Studies in the Scriptures*. Millions of copies were distributed, and it is interesting to note that these books were not sold in bookstores. The books were sold for a small price and were carried to the people door to door by colporteurs who were followers of Russell. Russell said there were 600 Christian people who had left all earthly business to distribute the books. There was much resistance and book burning.

Russell also wrote a number of other books: *Object and Manner of Our Lord's Return, Food for Thinking Christians, The Time Is at Hand,* and *The Photo Drama of Creation.* The *Watchtower* continues to be published biweekly. It is the basis of study used by the congregation. Another magazine published between *Watchtower* weeks is called *Awake.* This publication is a biweekly biased news and information magazine containing some articles of a nonreligious nature.

In 1910 the society formed the People's Pulpit Association of New York. In 1934 the name was changed to Watchtower Bible and Tract Society of New York, Inc. A British division is called the International Bible Student's Association.

Russell was married in 1879 to Maria Francis Ashley. She was active in the society and for years served as Russell's associate editor of the *Watchtower.* They were separated in 1897, and in 1913 Mrs. Russell sued for divorce on the grounds of "his conceit, egotism, domination and improper conduct in relation to other women." In the book *Jehovah of the Watchtower,* by Martin and Klann, the divorce proceedings are recorded along with the transcript of another trial in which Russell was involved. According to these court records, Russell was found to have deliberately lied under oath. The reader may wish to personally investigate these, so references are included in the appendix.

Russell died on October 31, 1916, a sick man on a train headed home from a speaking trip. He had had a busy sixty-four years. He personally wrote the charter for the society, established the branch offices, edited the *Watchtower* for over thirty years, wrote many books and delivered hundreds of sermons. Hours before his death he requested that his traveling companion, Menta Sturgeon, make him a Roman toga. This was done using bedsheets. Russell put on the toga, stood erect for a moment, then lay down on the couch.

In a biography on Russell written by J. F. Rutherford, the author said, "It was the official robe of higher magistrates, priests and of persons discharging vows and was worn on special occasions such as celebrating a triumph." Russell's associate considered him the "greatest religious leader since St. Paul." The biography also stated that Russell was not the founder of a new religion, that he made no claims of a special revelation from God but held it was God's direction for the Bible to be understood and, because Russell was fully consecrated to the Lord, he was committed to understanding.

It has been stated that some of the charges leveled against Russell by his wife were those of conceit, egotism, and domination. What did Russell think of himself? In the *Watchtower* of September 15, 1910, he made the following remarks about his book *Studies in the Scriptures:*

> Not only do we find that people cannot see the divine plan in studying the Bible by itself, but we see also that if anyone lays the *Scripture Studies* aside even after he has used them, after he has become familiar with them, after he has read them for ten years—if he lays them aside and ignores them and goes to the Bible alone, though he had understood his Bible for years, our experience shows that within two years he goes into darkness. On the other hand, if he had merely read the *Scripture Studies* with their references and had not read a page of the Bible as such, he would be in the light at the end of two years, because he would have the light of the Scriptures.

If these words be true, the Witnesses of today must be getting light elsewhere or else not getting light at all because those books have long been unavailable. The Watchtower Society itself removed these books from availability.

At Russell's passing, the organization was thrown into disarray and some of the officers battled for power. During one incident, as reported by MacMillan, a policeman was brought in to keep the peace.

Russell left a will containing his wishes for the operation of the society after his death. He directed that there be formed an editorial committee of five members, each one named by Russell, to be charged with responsibility for the *Watchtower.* His wish was that all articles appearing in the magazine have the unqualified approval of at least three of the five members. Controversial articles should be held for thought, prayer and discussion for three months before publication. He directed that the names of the editorial committee be published in each issue of the magazine. The society was pledged to publish no other periodicals. Of no small amount of interest is the fact that Russell's successor, J. F. Rutherford, was not named as one of the five, but his name was listed among a group of backup names. Of additional interest is the fact that Russell donated to the society all his voting shares through five other trustees; again Rutherford was not named. In fact, the will almost ignored him.

After his death, Russell was honored by his followers at an evening service of the headquarters staff. A speech was given by J. F. Rutherford in which he lifted Russell to the highest plane.

The "faithful and discreet slave" is an important term in Witness theology and will be dealt with in full later. However, it must be said here that Russell claimed to be, and was accepted by others to be, this "slave." This is vehemently denied by the modern Witnesses, but note the following quote from Rutherford's biography: "Thousands of the readers of Pastor Russell's writings believe that he filled the office of that faithful and wise servant, and that his great work was giving to the household of faith meat in due season. His modesty and humility precluded him from openly claiming this title, but he admitted as much in private conversations."

By whatever mechanism it actually happened, Joseph F. Rutherford replaced Russell as head of the Watchtower Society. He took office in 1917 and it appeared that he had his hands full. The "Russellites" were just that—totally devoted to Russell. They had to be assured that the sermons being published were in fact written by Russell. Many felt that his death marked the end of revelations. Recent Witness literature condemningly speaks of it as "creature worship." Many of the followers had expected the Lord to swoop down and get them in 1914 (even though they try to hide this fact). This led to considerable falling away. Rutherford set about to establish in their minds that the *organization* was the slave and to *deemphasize* Russell. Hence, the phrase "creature worship" was in fact referring to Russell. This

is interesting when just earlier Rutherford himself had proclaimed that Russell was the slave as previously quoted. There
was a major rebellion among the staff at the headquarters.

LOCAL CONGREGATIONS

It seems appropriate to turn at this point to a description of
the group of Witnesses in the local congregation. According to
William J. Schnell, in his book *Thirty Years a Watchtower Slave,*
the early congregations or ecclesias were far different from the
present Witness congregations. These were called "churches" at
times, a term the modern Witnesses avoid. For some reason
they'd rather use the title "Kingdom Hall" as the name of their
meeting place, apparently to distinguish themselves from anybody
else. But the early congregations sometimes were called by the
name "church." These early congregations were controlled locally
by "elders."

Schnell commented about brotherly love and fellowship in
the early congregations. Apparently it was his opinion that these
early Witnesses (not called by that name then) were Christian
as we would very much understand them today—open, loving,
charitable, community-minded people. They even had the option
of either using or not using the material in the society even as
late as 1921. The *Watchtower* of May 1, 1921, says,

> Each ecclesia or class is a body in itself, representing the
> Lord; and it has control over the affairs of that particular
> body. In accordance with the Scriptures, that ecclesia elects
> its elders, its deacons and other servants of the "church,"
> each one having his representative office to perform. We
> believe that all will agree that such is the "divine arrange-
> ment." The literature, when printed, is sent to the classes for
> distribution. No one is compelled to engage in the distri-
> bution of the literature, and if any individual feels that he
> cannot conscientiously distribute it he ought not do so.

Anyone familiar with the present-day Witnesses will recognize that the "divine arrangement" has changed. In a carefully calculated move the society took away local power from the congregations. Officers (even the title has been changed several times) must be selected (not necessarily elected) by headquarters. One cannot elect whether or not he will distribute the literature. It is required. Everything is controlled—from the officers, the offices, elections of officers, literature (no literature is tolerated unless it comes from the "slave"), to the titles and content of sermons—no deviation is allowed. The society even decides which songs to sing at meetings. *Individuality as seen in the early days of this movement has been eliminated and a singleness of thought and attitude now prevail; only the thoughts and attitudes sent down from headquarters are allowed.* Is this mind control?

OFFICES OF THE LOCAL GROUP

All Jehovah's Witnesses consider themselves to be ministers. The modern organization is careful to avoid terms used by others—such as "pastor," "church," "preacher"—although their founder himself was called "Pastor" Russell. The leader of the group is called the congregation servant. He is responsible for applying fully and to the greatest degree possible all the methods of work advised by the society. He is responsible for expansion of the Kingdom Witness, as explained in their book entitled *Qualified to Be Ministers*. He sees that all meetings are properly handled. He is on the watch and informed as to what is taking place. He realizes that this is an "educational organization," and its objective is to have not only the publisher but also the people of good will educated and trained. He must not use his own ideas; he follows the instructions of the organization. Other servants are the assistant servant, Bible study servant, magazine territory servant, literature servant, accounts servant, *Watchtower* study servant, minister school servant and book study conductor. (They may have changed these titles again since this book was written.)

MEETINGS

Meetings generally are held in small, sometimes rented, halls, but recently the Witnesses have built a number of small buildings and, in some instances, purchased the property. The meeting-place is called the Kingdom Hall. Several meetings are held each week. A principal meeting is usually held on Sunday and consists of two main parts. The public talk consists of a discourse by one of the male members or by a visiting Witness. He is rarely a skilled speaker, and most of the talks are monotonous, low key and, as a matter of fact, dull. The format sent down from headquarters is strictly followed. This may have much to do with the nature of the talk. The delivery usually is given in a soft, pleasant manner, intermingled with various scriptural references intended to substantiate the points being made. Almost all those people present are Jehovah's Witnesses, with the exception of one or two people called, "people of good will," perhaps with whom some of the members have been studying, and they have invited or brought to the meeting. These are usually people they have called upon in their homes. The messages have, for a hundred years, constantly warned that Armageddon is a breath away and the only place of safety is within the organization.

One or two songs are sung, perhaps accompanied by a piano or occasionally by tapes supplied by headquarters. Note that there is no music servant, and the singing is often disastrous. The song leader steps away from the microphone, so as not to be heard one supposes. Why don't they leave the music out altogether? It is evident that music is not important—a striking testimony to the absence of joy in this religion. Although the word "worship" is popular in their books, and they agree that the word means to bend before God, there is no kneeling and never any show of emotion.

After the lecture (sermon would not be a good word), the second meeting, an hour, is a study of the *Watchtower*. In the book entitled *Qualified to Be Ministers,* the importance of this meeting is clearly seen: "The *Watchtower* study deals with the principal publication of the faithful and discreet slave class" (meaning, of course, the organization). This study is therefore a key meeting of the congregation. When the *Watchtower* first arrives, the *Watchtower* study servant must make an immediate study of it. Each article has a specific purpose and notes the forward movement of the new world society. Each subject it discusses fits into the general theme of Jehovah's training through his organization.

The manner of study is also preplanned. Nothing is left to chance. To make sure that everyone understands the message of the *Watchtower* article according to the society, questions are printed at the bottom of the pages and the answers are given in the body of the article. The question is read by the reader; the leader and various audience members answer. If the answer is not the one desired, the subject is continued until the right answer is given or until the leader explains the correct answer. Then a person called a reader will read the particular paragraphs involved, then the next question is asked. So far, in both these meetings, the Bible is at best used as a reference book. There is never any direct Bible study in this or any other meeting. The format set down by the Witness organization for the congregation never includes study of the Bible itself. Remember what Russell said in *Studies in the Scriptures*?

Several additional meetings are held during the week. In the minister's school, they are trained to give talks. Much of the training deals with their house-to-house work, which is the backbone of the organization. The service meeting discusses housekeeping chores. All activity is controlled from headquarters with publications such as the *Informant* and other periodicals. Also, the local congregations are visited regularly by a representative from headquarters, usually the "circuit" servant who supervises several congregations. This visitor is kind but severe and a certain awesomeness accompanies his visit. He checks out congregations according to organization policy, and if things are amiss, he will set about promptly to correct them. One thing is totally evident— they all fear the wrath of this slave. Many deny this. To say this frustrates them, but the truth is easily discerned.

Other meetings include the congregation book study and the neighborhood book study. At these less formal meetings (refreshments may be served in the home meetings) one of the myriad of hardbound books is studied in *Watchtower* fashion. The questions are provided on the pages and the answer is in the text. Again, the Bible itself is not studied. In fact, it is so important that I emphasize again that never in their history has the Bible itself been studied. This movement began through the writings of a man and his interpretations of the Bible. In the hundred-year history of the Witness movement, never has the Bible itself been studied. It is actually at best a reference book, secondary to the publications of the "slave."

Saturday and Sunday mornings are popular days for house-to-house work. Everyone must participate in this. Weekdays also are utilized by some. Years ago, there were publishers who carried a phonograph to play a record at the door. But this has been discarded for some time, and the Witnesses now have a brief, rehearsed speech that they may have folded up on a small piece of paper inside one of their books, and they have a satchel full of literature. Success is based on the number of books placed, and there is usually a special offer.

Records of this work are kept in great detail, noting the hours spent, people visited, meetings held, callbacks made, and so on. Witnesses have been known to utilize certain tricks, such as leaving many magazines at the doors of apartments. They may also give away books instead of assessing the small charge. Witnesses pay for their literature at a small discount, and then it's up to them to recover their cost. Hours spent are carefully reported. Almost all of these materials are sold at a low price, being first sold to the publishers. A look inside the home of Witnesses has revealed at times stacks of literature that were never distributed.

Joseph Franklin Rutherford, the second president of the Watchtower, was born of a Baptist family in 1869 in Missouri. He studied law and was admitted to the bar at the age of twenty-two. He did have some appointments as a judge and became known as Judge Rutherford. He experienced considerable resistance from within the organization, and much infighting took place for power but Rutherford was adequate for the job. He pushed out a final work of Russell's, the seventh and last volume of *Studies in the Scriptures*. In this book he presented Russell's interpretation of the Book of Revelation. Later he wrote a book giving his own views, but in Russell's seventh volume (compiled by two leaders in the movement under Rutherford's presidency) there was unleashed a vicious attack on what he called "Babylon," which included all other organized religions. Later Rutherford himself would pick up the theme.

"Babylon," the "church nominal," was called an abomination in the sight of the Lord as seen in the pro-Witness book by Marley Cole. The seventh volume made the claim that religion, politics, and commerce were tied together in some manner so as to be a single organization headed by the devil himself. Babylon later was called Christendom. This was only the start. Rutherford wrote more books on the same theme, and this theme continues to the present. A footnote at this point is that there is considerable evidence that the Watchtower Society is coming out with new views again, which is consistent with its history.

An absolutely unbelievable hardcover book was released in 1978 entitled *Our Incoming World Government, God's Kingdom*. This may very well be their worst work and possibly a contribution toward the Communist cause, even though printed by non-Communists. The message to the hypnotized followers of the Watchtower Society is boldly and most clearly seen in this book which states, "The day of the long-promised world government is dawning." By now the devout Witness finds the words "Jehovah," "faithful and discreet slave," "organization," and now "world government" to all be one and the same. The frantic message that strikes fear in their hearts is clear and plain. There is no place for safety outside the organization. The organization must be the base. The organization is Jehovah.

William Schnell, in his *Thirty Years a Watchtower Slave*, described the events as Rutherford assumed power. The First World War was beginning when Rutherford assumed leadership. The stand taken by the society against governments and against war soon led them into trouble with the Canadian and American governments. Schnell says that the seemingly antiwar policy of the society helped to reunite the splintered society. The organization in New York was legally dissolved. Rutherford and the other directors of the society were arrested. They were tried, convicted, and imprisoned in the Federal Penitentiary in Atlanta, Georgia.

After the war ended, society members petitioned governors and congressmen, and the convicted men were freed and exonerated. It must be said here that only in America could such be accomplished, but they had used America for their cause. Russell had told his followers to join the army if they had to and to take nonfighting jobs if possible. But Rutherford's followers selected jail rather than serving in the military in any capacity. They were sure this was the will of Jehovah.

Judge Rutherford took over the society. He wrote many, many books, and the theme of us vs. them, antieverybody, was developed even more. At first Rutherford continued Russell's books and ideas to keep his predecessor's followers in the fold. The slave changed from Russell to the organization. Slowly Russellites became Rutherfordites. Rutherford moved forward very successfully. He appointed new board members and organized positions of authority, and he put down the internal rebellion.

Had Russell preferred a man named A. H. MacMillan to be president rather than Rutherford? There is evidence to suggest this possibility, in MacMillan's own book entitled *Faith on the March*. But Rutherford was president and he ruled, and it was Rutherford who gave the members their popular name, Jehovah's Witnesses at a convention in Columbus, Ohio, in 1931.

During the ten years preceding this date, Rutherford was writing books, changing some of Russell's interpretation of Scripture ("getting new light," they call it). Books were sold by the million, and even at their relatively small prices, the money rolled in and they were well capitalized. (The organization never gives a financial accounting to anyone, not even to their membership.) Schnell notes that during the twenties the Witnesses changed from being interested in what they had previously termed "the Christian walk in the spirit as new creation," to an interest in growth, quotas and book sales. This interest is still with them today.

As previously stated, Rutherford wrote many books, and he claimed authorship proudly. Each book contained pages advertising his other books. But every book also contained the urgent reminder that time had run out, Armageddon was almost here, in every book, every moment, of the existence of the Watchtower Society. *Creation* described his view of how God made the world. *Preservation* explained the Books of Esther and Ruth. *Prophecy* explained prophecy. Yet, notice that none of these prophecies was ever found to be true. (More about this later.) *Government* was the "indisputable evidence showing that the peoples of earth shall have a religious government and explains the manner of its establishment." *Light* told the "physical facts set forth showing fulfillment of the Revelation." A point of interest about these books is that terms such as "cross" and "crucifixion," and pictures of Christ on a typical cross and references to the Blood of Christ, are frequently seen. But the Witnesses have a different view on these subjects today.

One of Rutherford's books requires considerable comment. In the book called *Preparation,* the reader gets an idea of the fantastic imagination of the mind of this man. It is incredible that people would place credence in such material. For example, in this book, Rutherford divides people into various classes claiming, of course, scriptural support. Note the following list: Judah class, p. 49; faithful and discreet slave class, p. 33; evil servant class, p. 141; man of sin, son of perdition, p. 199; clergy class, p. 199; elected elder class, p. 199; Zechariah class, p. 207; faithful servant class, p. 214; idol-worshipping class, p. 214; worthless servant class, p. 218; they that do the looking class, p. 231; they that do the piercing class, p. 231; sanctuary class, p. 237; temple class, p. 237; detestable class, p. 251; Sampson class, p. 253; howling class, p. 265; slothful servant class, p. 267; evil servant class, p. 267; and God's approved class, p. 269.

Could all of these classes of people be placed in one of two categories, Christian or non-Christian? In other words, how can you deal with this? Could anyone allow his mind to accept these teachings? Yes, thousands of people. Rutherfordites . . . Jehovah's Witnesses do.

Inventing classes was a forte of the organization, especially under Rutherford. At first Russell was "the faithful and discreet slave," then the organization itself suddenly became the slave—called a "class." Now the slave, being more than one, of course necessitated a different interpretation of Matthew 24. There is more to add to the confusion. For a time, there was a Mordecai-Naomi class, limited to 144,000 plus Jesus, making 144,001. Then came the Ruth-Esther class. Then came the Jonadabs, who just might receive an earthly reward if they would support the "faithful and wise servant class," which was also called "Jehovah's Witnesses" (*Riches,* 1939). Those three classes are or were what we now call Jehovah's Witnesses. But there is more confusion. The 144,000 are also called the "remnant." When the membership grew beyond 144,000, this obviously meant no more could join or else another class must be formed. Well, of course, another class was formed. These class members all understand that they will not receive eternal life in heaven, but if they do good work, by all means remain in the organization, they *may* gain eternal life on a new earth. Do you recall reading this in the Bible? You don't?

There are said to be about 10,000 members of the remnant still living on earth. As they die, they instantly are transmitted to heaven. It is very difficult to find in Witness literature just how God selected them and what they do. The "meat in due season," meaning the books and instructions, supposedly comes from God through the remnant or slave, but what part does one play who lives in Mexico and has never communicated with the Brooklyn headquarters? Only the most gullible members would believe that the people they know personally in the congregation who are now supposedly members of the remnant have ever had a part whatsoever in the supplying of food. A person is recognized to be of the earthly class, if he does not participate in the emblems of the Lord's evening meal. Apparently God tells people directly if they are members of the remnant and whether or not they may participate. The Watchtower Society's literature does not make this clear at all. However, we know that some of those who have fallen away reportedly have been members of the remnant.

Of the hodgepodge concerning the doctrine of the remnant, this seems to be the summary of it. In Russell's *Divine Plan of the Ages* he wrote of the fact that the Christian Church, the Body of Christ, is an exception to God's general plan for mankind, that God not only foresaw the fall of the race into sin, but He also predetermined the justification, sanctification and glorification of this class which, during the gospel age, had been called out of the world to be conformed to the image of God's Son (p. 193).

To be partakers of the divine nature and to be fellow heirs with Christ Jesus to the millennial kingdom for the establishment of universal righteousness and peace, Russell explained that this meant that the Church of Jesus Christ was so elected, but this did not mean that each individual member was included. At that time, we must remember the Christian Church was not looked upon by Russell as exclusively Jehovah's Witnesses. He called them a little flock selected by God on the basis of severe trials of faith, obedience and the sacrifice of earthly privileges even to death. These called ones first were Jews; then Gentiles were included. They were born of the Holy Spirit (the term was capitalized by Witnesses then; it isn't now).

Russell called this the narrow way—sacrificial living. Some of those called didn't do a good job but didn't wholly forsake the law—so they had to be purified by the "fire of affliction." They gain everlasting spiritual life equal to that of angels but lose the prize—immortality. Their position is less glorious than that of the little flock. There is also, said Russell, a broad road that one travels deluded by Satan. This comes later and is easier to achieve. However, this highway of holiness only leads to human perfection on earth, not immortality. This road is easier because it is not a narrow, steep, rugged, difficult, edged byway but a way especially prepared for easy travel, specially arranged for the convenience and comfort of the travelers. Verses eight and nine of Isaiah 35 show that it is a public road open to all the redeemed, to every man. Russell continues:

Every man for whom Christ died who will recognize and avail himself of opportunities and blessing purchased by the Precious Blood, you may go upon this highway of holiness to the grand goal of perfect restitution to human perfection and everlasting life.

Russell said the broad road was soon to be opened. These "revelations" were in Russell's book, *Divine Plan of the Ages,* published in 1886, and apparently it introduced the idea of the little flock or heavenly class. In 1933, Rutherford gave his view on the remnant. By now, he was presenting his own theology, and wherever it differed from Russell's earlier view, Rutherford simply said his version was correct. (This is undoubtedly one of the reasons why so much of the doctrine of the Witnesses is very difficult to follow.)

In the book *Preparation* (p. 287), Rutherford identifies God's organization on earth as the "city" (more prophecy fulfilled). He was describing the period just after Russell died, when there was turmoil within the organization. Those members who split from the city he called—yes—a class. They began the evil slave class. Do you see? Rutherford's group had become the faithful and discreet slave class, and those ex-Witnesses who opposed Rutherford were named the evil class. They were "raped . . . and their virginity lost" (p. 287), who fell away and yielded to the world.

In 1918, during the time of the assault made by Satan's agents, the people then forming God's organization on earth were separated into two companies or divisions. Using a quote from Zechariah which says, "and half of the city shall go forth into captivity," Rutherford explained that the organization symbolized by the city was divided into two halves. One half was the evil servant class and the other was used by God to make up the faithful and wise servant class. The evil servants were cut off completely from God's organization, but the faithful and wise remnant would not be. The ones who were cut off could never be restored to the city. This, undoubtedly, was intended to frighten those who would challenge the leaders. On the other hand, the remnant, whose members maintained their integrity, virgin purity and cleanliness, God declares "shall not be cut off from the city" (p. 290).

Rutherford continues that no other interpretation of this prophecy could be correct. In *Preparation* (p. 291), he makes clear how this should be viewed:

> It is the faithful remnant cleansed and made a part of the temple organization that constitutes the people of God taken out for His name and upon which people God bestows His name and sends them forth to be his witnesses; and to this class the testimony of Jesus Christ. It is against this faithful remnant that Satan gathers his forces to make war.

This quote is very important in understanding Rutherford's view.

On page 292 Rutherford says that there on Mount Zion God gathered them to himself, the entire 144,000 members of His body, including the faithful remnant on the earth, all of whom are joining in the "victory song of praise to Jehovah and His mighty anointed ones."

Do you see the point made here? The society, by its own proclamation, was God's only earthly organization. This means, of necessity, that the doctrine and interpretation maintained by Rutherford, the supreme leader, was absolute and authoritative. Those who rose to question or challenge him became evil slaves separated forever from God. No second chance was available for them. After this cleansing of the temple, the remaining remnant became the only people upon whom God would bestow His name, fulfilling the prophecy of Zechariah. Satan now (in 1933) gathers his forces to make war (Armageddon) against this remnant.

Rutherford discovered from Revelation that a passage concerning 144,000 Jews (in his mind) describes this remnant, taking one portion of Scripture literally, another symbolically. Notice the requirement he set for these people to become members. They were the ones who stayed with and believed in the organization, and they that would be sent forth were the same ones.

Then Rutherford said (p. 251) that *God stopped the World War in 1918 for the sake of the remnant so that they could begin preparing for Armageddon!* Read this for yourself. Well, we need one more class and here it is, the Jonadabs. Pages 304-305 tell about them. The "truth," called *Living Waters,* goes out from the organization. The remnant is commanded to invite whomever they wish to take of this water. Some of this water is taken by a class called Jonadabs. These are the ones the remnant was able to reach before Armageddon. The rest of the world could not receive the truth until after Armageddon. These last people evidently were not Christians, and Rutherford did not make their reward clear. They were not brothers, in other words, not organization members. This is how Rutherford explained the working of God and the justice of God. One thing is sure—the organization, as always, is the only ark of safety.

Much can be seen about the to and fro doctrine set forth in the voluminous books written by Rutherford. For example, today's Witnesses are told that Christ did not die on a cross but on a torture stake. The importance of this is seen when it is realized that they claim that Jesus was just a perfect man while on earth, and obvious efforts have been made in their literature to lower the position of Jesus. But in his books Rutherford included pictures of Jesus on a typical cross. For example, on page 295 of the book *Creation,* the picture is entitled "Crucifixion."

Constantly, the books, as well as all other Witness materials, have emphasized the urgency of the time. The end was always the next thing to happen. The book *Light* (Book II, 1930, p. 9) says that the end time is at hand. God will now shortly use Armageddon to completely vindicate his name (p. 17). The beginning of the pouring out of the third bowl dates from July 25, 1924 (p. 25). And we are now approaching that great battle (p. 292). This is an example of the urgency that is constantly and consistently expressed by the Witnesses, as well as their prediction of dates.

Rutherford's greatest publication blunder was a book called *Children.* It has been the custom of the society to release an important new book each year at major conventions. For the release of *Children,* Rutherford arranged a highly staged activity. Children present at the assembly were lined up. Cartons of the books were opened and the children were given copies of it during a great ceremony. Carmen Giolotti, an ex-member of the 144,000, was one of the children, and he reported on the receipt of his copy and the accompanying excitement it brought. Then the book was purchased by the thousands attending the convention and then subsequently made available to others. In this book, copyrighted in 1941, Rutherford presented a story of John Alden and Eunice Rogers. In tender terminology the story tells that John goes away to college and Eunice to seminary for women. After completing their schooling, they are together again four years later and discussing their future plans. They intend to marry and are discussing very seriously the circumstances of their future. John has come upon what was called "a number of books all published by this same publishing society which claimed to be of great aid in the study of the Bible." So they agreed to study one hour a day while they contemplated their future. Then, as the chapters of the book unfold, John and Eunice learn the Watchtower Society's interpretation as of 1941.

Now here is mind-bending, perhaps at its very best or worst. This book teaches John and Eunice that Armageddon is imminent. Notice these statements from the book: "My choice, Eunice, dear, is to serve Jehovah and his theocratic government. And I now declare aloud that I make this my choice—will you choose to go with me?" And Eunice answers that she would choose nothing else. And then he tells her that some sweet day they will have children and then they will be greatly blessed.

In another section, John tells Eunice that the studies they've had together have been a great blessing to him, and he goes on to say that he's "found a number of books there which were evidently provided by the Lord." And he tells her that Armageddon surely is near, that by faith they could now see the theocracy, and that from now on they should have their hearts' devotion fixed on the theocracy knowing that soon they would journey together in the earth. He says that his hope is that in a few years their marriage could be consummated. By the Lord's grace they could have children but they could defer this marriage until lasting peace came to the earth. They feel they should add nothing to their burden but to be free to serve the theocracy.

The word "theocracy" and the importance of theocracy are repeated several times in the book. John says that at this time it would be burdensome to have a family, but after Armageddon it won't. And so John sums it up by telling Eunice that he has made his decision, that he will shun politics, religion, and commerce and even avoid the city. And he and Eunice were committed forever to *the theocracy!* This makes some story. The story of John and Eunice was published in 1941. If John were twenty then, he would be sixty-one now in 1982—a little old to have children and a marriage.

Armageddon did not come as Rutherford indicated. How many young people were wrongfully influenced at that time? What effect did this have on their lives? What effect did this have on their admonition from the Bible to fill the earth? And what happened to the book? Can you find a copy of it today? If you wrote a letter to the Watchtower Society, would they send you a copy of this book? Would they dare tell you the error in this book? Is this organization they call God's organization dealing honestly with error? Is it not a very serious thing to misinform your followers? Would the society say it really made a mistake there? No. But what about the unyielding devotion to this theocracy? It was not stated as devotion to God himself but to the theocracy. Who is this? What is this? The theocracy was the Watchtower Society. The theocracy still is the Watchtower Society.

A small hardcover released in 1977 entitled *Our Coming World Government, God's Kingdom* further describes a theocracy. In chapter one it's called the next rulership for all the earth. A form of government is described in great detail. Now two important points become evident. No Scripture is cited in the entire first chapter. Significantly, God is not mentioned until the last two pages, but the point intended is clearly made that the day of the long-promised world government is dawning. It states that within this generation government will rise. All the subjects of the world government will understand one another because the world government takes away all language barriers. The one language all speak from mutual understanding is the language recognized and used by the world government. But now in the new order under world government, there's but one set of laws for all people. The world government has an expert weather bureau that is never wrong. The world government engages in repair work of the bodies and minds of all its subjects. The world government takes over full management of human affairs.

How able is this new government? This new government can rightly be proud of all living subjects under it. The world government has one mind. The world government does not need any tombstone. The world government wants the whole earth comfortably filled with its subjects. Their faith and practice are what the world government approves of.

It is almost impossible not to inject here a reflection of the society's overwhelming history of error. This is the saddest statement of the whole book: "It is human nature to worship something and the world government is fulfilling that need." *Read that one again!* The book relates the world government to God. That's what it says—God's world government. The intent of these twenty-two paragraphs cannot in any way be mistaken. The inference is clear—the world government is the Watchtower Society. Fear, a common finding among cults, is ever-present among members of the society. Are we talking about God, the omnipotent, omniscient, omnipresent One—or about omniscient, omnipotent, omnipresent *government*? Does the Bible describe God in terms of an impersonal government? The world government will, the world government shall, etc. Doesn't careful scrutiny show that the emphasis is on the government rather than on the only God? Yes, it does and that is the intention.

The Witness movement became enraptured with the idea of a government, which they call God's government, but beyond this, God has no part other than the use of His name. The government is a figment of the mind of Rutherford that has been continued by his successors, revealed in cloudy, changing explanations, such as the 144,000 of Revelation and the faithful and discreet slave in Matthew. The truth is that the movement needs a government (meaning, of course, the leaders themselves) to keep its brainwashed followers in line. The alternative would be to do what they pretend to do—follow the Bible and the God of the Bible. Without their books, they have no religion. Without their books, they too would have to follow God in the Bible. The greatest mystery concerning the movement is the failure of their members to check on the "food" they are given. This is surely mind control. They are convinced that the society can do no wrong for they refuse to deal with evidence that might cause them to question. They simply elect to go on in the society, whatever!

The organization adopted the name Jehovah's Witnesses under Rutherford in 1931 at a convention. As a matter of fact, he decided on their name. Rutherford took a verse from Isaiah 43:10, where God told the Israelites that they were His witnesses, and he applied the Scripture to the movement. So in 1931, they officially became Jehovah's Witnesses.

Rutherford is quoted in Marley Cole's book *Jehovah's Witnesses*: "By the grace of the Lord Jesus Christ and of our Heavenly Father, we joyfully receive and bear the name which the mouth of Jehovah God has named and given to us, to wit, Jehovah's Witnesses" (p. 101). So, this was apparently another fulfillment of prophecy. Also, it would have to mean that Isaiah 43:10 had two meanings: one for the Israelites and one for the Russellites. In the fifties they also called themselves the New World Society but seem to have abandoned this term.

Children was Rutherford's last book. He died in 1942 after twenty-five years in sole charge of the organization. Russell established this peculiar movement clearly in rebellion against organized religion, but Rutherford developed it. He salvaged the failing religion when Russell died.

A prolific writer, Rutherford attacked the enemy. He invented terms like Christendom, divided the world into classes, and fired up his followers to a zealous heat against Babylon, which he defined as Britain and America. With great skill he used his books to tell followers what the Bible meant. He explained Russell's errors and told his people whom to like and whom to hate. His early writings recognized as Christians at least a few people outside the organization, such as Russell's parents, but by the time of his end, he had successfully and clearly divided his followers from all the rest of the world.

Rutherford was brash in his writings. He stated matter of factly that in 1925 the "ancient worthies," namely Moses and Abraham, were to return to live and rule on this earth. He even bought a house for them called Beth Sarim. After they did not return to earth, Rutherford still continued to predict their coming but just less exactly. Was he correct or even nearly correct? That was fifty-four years ago. Rutherford was living in the house at the time of his own death. The worthies had not come to occupy it so the house finally was sold.

3

Doctrine and Prophecy

At one time in their hundred-year history, the Witnesses declared that theirs was not a religion. Two of their books were entitled *Religion a Snare and a Racket* and *What Has Religion Done for Mankind?* In the Witnesses' book entitled *The New World,* published in 1942, religion is defined: "Religion is, therefore, scripturally defined as everything that is against doing the will of God. It is a form of worship but which worship is given to a false God and hence given to a creature. It is the exact opposite of the worship of God."

One can tell the contents of the book from the title—*Religion a Snare and a Racket.* This book was a scathing attack, a real blast at all religions, especially Catholicism and Protestantism, calling them collectively a snare and a racket. If you can obtain a copy of this book, the bitter, deliberate, planned attacks made by the society can be clearly recognized. So it is quite clear that strong efforts were made by this society over a number of years to establish their organization as a direct opposite to any and all religions. The Watchtower Society and religion were to be understood to be at opposite ends of the spectrum. So they defined religion as everything that is against the will of God. In other words, there is religion on the one hand and the society on the other—complete opposites. Now, here is a peculiar finding. Since Rutherford, in more recent years, the Witnesses now say they are, after all, a religion. After the feverish attacks and the name-calling, it is very surprising that they reached a point at which they found it advantageous after all to be called a religion.

27

28

In fact, they now have decided that they are *the* religion, the *only* pure religion. Well, wouldn't you just know they also discovered a new definition for religion? No longer "anything opposed to God," religion has become "a form of worship without regard to whether it is true or false" (*What Has Religion Done for Mankind?* p. 10). Ah, now that the word was redefined, it would be possible for the organization to be a religion after all. This new position allowed the society to capitalize on the very word they had so bitterly denounced. People who felt they should be religious could now be so and still be Jehovah's Witnesses. Clearly this allowed for more new members.

The above example reveals a demonstration of the ever-changing positions of the society. The same applies to their doctrine. It is not the purpose of this book to present details of the error of their doctrine because this has been done in several well-researched, honest investigations which are all available in print (see list in appendix). These books are highly recommended. Many are scholarly works on the various biblical attitudes and interpretations of the Jehovah's Witnesses.

It is the purpose of this book to show how their doctrine has been totally changed in some cases, other times partially changed, reinterpreted according to the events at hand, sometimes denied and oftentimes ignored. In Russell's and Rutherford's days, when they were the faithful and discreet slaves, they made numerous prophetic predictions that were said to be undeniably true. Had these things come to pass, truly they would have been prophets. In their own words they explained how to recognize a true prophet. In their book called *Aid to Bible Understanding,* the point is made that a true prophet is usually identified by the fact that things foretold would come to pass. At times it has been difficult for them to explain just how a fulfillment occurred since this did not happen as they had predicted. They have come to admit, to a degree at least, that errors have been made. But could error be made in true revealed prophecy? Was any other prophecy erroneous? Was prophecy in the Bible erroneous?

Please keep in mind the Witnesses' claims that the Watchtower Society is, and has been for the past hundred years, the only channel to God. This means that when the society is off the track, the world must wait to hear truth from God since there is no other source. But how could God's only channel get off the track? Think of this—would Almighty God allow His organization to cause people to accept blood transfusions, for instance, until the year 1945 and not allow this for people after that year?

THE FAITHFUL AND DISCREET SERVANT CLASS

1. "Whom has the Lord used to thus serve the church meat in due season? Everyone who desires to state the facts must answer that he used Charles Taze Russell." (*Watchtower,* 12/1/22, p. 376).
2. "Pastor Russell is that servant" (*Watchtower,* 11/1/19, p. 323).
3. "The Watchtower unhesitatingly proclaimed Brother Russell as that faithful and wise servant" (*Watchtower,* 3/1/27, p. 67).
4. "Without a doubt, Pastor Russell filled the office for which the Lord provided and about which he spoke and was, therefore, that wise and faithful servant" (*Harp of God,* J. F. Rutherford, 1927 ed., p. 239).

When Russell died, the slave changed:

> Those whom the Lord finds to be faithfully devoted to Him, and who are making the Kingdom interests paramount to everything else, He approves; and all such collectively He designated that faithful and wise servant over all of His goods namely, all of His Kingdom interests on earth. Concerning such it is written, verily I say unto you that He shall make him ruler over all his goods (Matt. 24:45-47).

"In contrast therewith, the Scriptures mention an evil servant class that is made up of the ones disapproved by the Lord because they have not shown a proper appreciation of God's Kingdom" (*Government,* J. F. Rutherford, 1928, p. 192). Recall now that Rutherford had as recently as the year before (*Harp of God,* 1927) stated that Russell was the servant. Now, in the above reading, he explains that all of his followers who do right *collectively* constitute the servant. We also recall now that they were still a small group and wouldn't be called by the name Jehovah's Witnesses until 1931. Now, notice this carefully: in the same book, Rutherford explains that this servant group and the remnant are the same. On page 211 the remnant is defined:

What came to pass on natural Israel foreshadowed what would come to pass at the end of the world upon the professed followers of Christ and clearly shows that there would be a remnant at this time [end of the world]. A remnant is that which remains after the larger number has been taken away. That means that, after the shaking has taken place and after the gathering out from the Kingdom, mentioned by the Lord Jesus, if you would remain true and faithful unto God and would delight to do His will, then such would be moved wholly by an unselfish devotion to Him. That class constitutes the remnant. It is the remnant whom the Lord designates as that faithful and wise servant to whom he commits all his goods for government interests upon the earth (Matt. 24:45; Isa. 42:1-6). It is the faithful remnant that delights to obey the commands of the Lord in making proclamation of the Good News. If one who is anointed of the Lord fails to be of the remnant class it is his own fault and is due to pride, indifference, or negligence. These are the ones whom he uses to do his great and marvelous work. They are small in number.

To complete this doctrine, we must find out what Rutherford meant by anointed because today's Witnesses have a different understanding. Rutherford defines the term "anointed" (p. 207):

During the past fifty years a goodly number have been brought to a knowledge of present truth and have made a consecration to do God's will and, having been accepted in Christ, have received the anointing for a place in the kingdom. Some of these were by nature better endowed than others and more apt to teach and have been placed in the position of elders of the various ecclesias.

Rutherford goes on to explain that some of the anointed don't preach as they are told, having preferred to follow their own wisdom (p. 207), but he doesn't exactly call them bad guys. A summary of his interpretation is found on page 217: "Jehovah then addressing his servant class, the anointed ones who are called to be his witnesses and who constitute the remnant . . ."

Of major importance is the fact that at this point in their history the "other sheep class" has not yet been formed. Rutherford's impression is clearly that God formed an organization through Christ all bound for heaven, that many had already been taken off the earth, that a small remnant of the organization was left on earth that constitutes his followers, who were anointed into Christ and that included all the organization, and only these people would gain a heavenly reward. He also said that if one who could be anointed and be of the remnant failed to do so, it was his own fault—due to pride, indifference, or negligence. So, evidently he felt that if people wanted to work and become a member of the remnant, they had that privilege. Of course, that view is also changed today. But only these people would gain a heavenly reward. People who listened to them and converted to society teachings could possibly gain an earthly reward.

Witnesses, this is certainly not what you're being taught today. Before you lock your mind in defense—wait! Obtain a copy of the book entitled *Government*. Ask your congregation servant if you may study it. He will surely say no, but study it anyway. Seeing is believing. Will you see? This definition of the servant meant the organization. No mention of 144,000 or any other specific number can be found.

AND THE SLAVE CHANGED AGAIN

1. "The idea adopted by many was that C. T. Russell himself was a faithful and wise servant."
2. "He never claimed to be such, however, he did continue to edit the *Watchtower*. He organized Zion Watchtower Tract Society. He authored and published six volumes of *Studies in the Scriptures* as well as many other booklets and delivered innumerable public lectures. It cannot be successfully dis-

puted that till he died in 1916, he lovingly served as part of the faithful and discreet slave class. However the sense of appreciation and indebtedness toward Russell moved many of his associates to view him as the fulfillment of the faithful and discreet slave."

What is happening here? Russell is about to be put on the shelf and his role markedly diminished. The above is quoted from *God's Kingdom of 1,000 Years,* published in 1963. On the same page the subject of the servant continues. Next comes one of the best examples of the dishonest journalism employed by the society. Explaining further that many viewed Russell as the servant, the book says: "This view was prominently featured in the book published in July 1917 by People's Pulpit Association of New York. This book was called *The Finished Mystery . . .* on its publishers page, the book was the posthumous work of Pastor Russell. Such a book and religious attitude tended to establish a religious sect centered around a man." The deception attempted here is to pretend that the book was published by an organization outside the society and that it was not a good, honest work. But the real truth is found in the *Watchtower* dated December 15, 1917. Well, *The Finished Mystery* turned out to be the last book Russell had been working on and was completed by followers under Rutherford and other society leaders who authorized that two men named Woodruff and Fisher would finish Russell's book. The *Watchtower* says,

It was prepared under the direction of the Watchtower Bible and Tract Society and will be seen by reference to the preface. The name of the society likewise appears on the outside of the cover. Upon the title page appears the name of the International Bible Student's Association which has likewise appeared with title pages of other volumes for several years and the copyright was given the name of the People's Pulpit Association. Thus, it is seen that all three of the corporations which jointly are used to carry on the harvest work participated in the putting out of the book . . .

Thus is presented unmistakable proof of dishonest journalism shown by the Watchtower Society. The *1973 Yearbook of Jehovah's Witnesses* presents the People's Pulpit Association as if they were an organization other than themselves. How could God's organization lie to its followers? When the book originally was published all this was said in the *Watchtower* to impress upon people that the work was, in fact, Russell's work. And it was, in fact, the work of the society. They emphasized this by saying that all three of their organizations had their stamp of approval on it. Yet later, when they wanted to diminish Russell, they tried to pretend that the People's Pulpit Association was some foreign outfit that published the book. How could God's organization lie to its followers? They did it on the strength that the information would not and could not be verified. Also, forty-five years had passed since 1928 to the year 1973. But paragraph 33 on page 34 finishes off the matter. Here they explain that in 1927 any remaining stocks of all the volumes of *Studies in the Scriptures* were disposed of. Isn't it perfectly clear by now? Russell was put to rest and relegated to a lesser position in the history of the organization.

It now becomes apparent that many Witnesses don't know the real truth, the real history of their organization. The "servant" became the organization. Or rather, and more correctly, the servant became a small portion of the organization which is now called the remnant. There are supposedly 10,000 members of the remnant on earth, but for certain only a small handful of these are handing out the "food." No, they occupy a very small space because the food, in fact, comes from a small group of men in Brooklyn, New York. All the food comes from this single source. These are the real remnant. These are the real "slaves." These are the real minds who furnish the spiritual food for all the millions of Jehovah's Witnesses.

4

The Worship of Jesus Christ

For a number of years, during most of the Witnesses' history, Jesus has occupied a position secondary to "the only true God," Jehovah. They say that in some way, Jesus is "a" god, but not "the" God. The Witnesses are told that Jesus is important. He did pay the ransom but he was not with God in the beginning. He was the first created thing or being, then he helped God create everything else. Jesus was only one of millions of sons of God selected to come to earth for the ransom because God knew him and felt Jesus would perform well. (Don't believe they are taught this? Read about Jesus Christ in the book entitled *Aid to Bible Understanding.*)

The Witnesses now teach that Jesus was only a perfect man. He was not crucified, their recent books say; he was impaled on a torture stake. In contrast to their earlier books, with pictures depicting the Crucifixion and Christ on a cross, in more recent years the Witnesses have changed their terminology, for they avoid the use of the words "crucified" and "cross," saying that Jesus was "impaled on a torture stake." They also note a major difference about the significance of a stake meaning something different from a cross.

Witness teaching regarding Jesus Christ almost entirely ignores the New Testament. Even though they have published hundreds of books, there has never been one on the life of Christ. Jesus is, at best, selectively discussed. Witnesses are taught that his spirit was resurrected but his body was not. They say that he did a good job on earth, and Jehovah gave him immortality

34

whereas the rest of us only get eternal life. Jesus has already returned to earth either in 1874 or in 1914 (whichever date you want to accept), but he didn't actually return. He had a coming but he didn't come, but he is present, which means that he is not actually here but has turned his attention, as the Witnesses say, toward the earth. This turning of attention means by their doctrinal interpretation his "coming." Witnesses may do obeisance to Jesus, but they must not worship him. This also is a modern change from the earlier, original organizing doctrine of the Witness movement. Most members of the Watchtower Society do not know that their incorporating charter states that its purpose is the worship of Almighty God and Jesus Christ. By now we see that the Watchtower Society's literature varies.

Did the Witnesses ever worship Jesus? "Question . . . was he really worshipped or is the translation faulty? Answer . . . yes, we believe our Lord while on earth was really worshipped and properly so . . . it was proper for our Lord to receive worship" (*Watchtower*, July 15, 1898).

"He was the object of unreproved worship even when a babe, by the wisemen who came to see the newborn king . . . he never reproved any for acts of worship offered to himself . . . had Christ not been more than man, the same reason would have prevented him from receiving worship . . ." (*Watchtower*, Oct. 1, 1880, p. 144; quoted by Edmond Gruss in his *We Left Jehovah's Witnesses, A Non-Prophet Organization*).

In the charter of the Watchtower Society of Pennsylvania, Article II, the purposes of the Watchtower Society are given. One of these purposes states: "And for public Christian worship of Almighty God and Christ Jesus." Is this unaltered statement clear? Can the meaning be doubted? This document is now a matter of record, but wait—today's Witnesses know that they are taught not to worship Jesus, being allowed only to do him obeisance. This appears to have created something of a problem for Witnesses in recent years, particularly among the older Witnesses, who are observant of the changes. They have been told that the word "worship" has different degrees and meanings, so that some of the people when confronted would say, well, yes, we do worship Jesus, but we don't worship him in the same way we worship God. I'm sure this is a difficult thing for the membership to understand that one can worship in different degrees. Nevertheless, this is what is currently being told and very likely is what has led to this situation of worship on the one hand and obeisance on the other.

It is doubtful that any of the present-day members of the Watchtower Society know their original charter included the worship of Jesus because the society will not tell them what the charter says. Rather, here goes the journalism again. The *1969 Yearbook of Jehovah's Witnesses* quotes the charter thus: "And for public Christian worship of Almighty God . . ." Was something left out? Well, the charter is quoted again in the *Watchtower* of December 15, 1971 (p. 760): "And for public Christian worship of Almighty God (through) Christ Jesus." One thing is certain here, some man or men in the society hierarchy knew that he or they were altering these articles and the purpose is very obvious. This is deception. This is dishonest representation of their own literature. The Witnesses were changing again. Earlier, they cut Russell down to a lower position; now they've done this to Jesus Christ. May the reader consider deeply and soberly this information. Challenge it thoroughly. Demand proof. Your life is at stake and all the lives you lead into your organization.

5

That Big Year in Witness History—1914—
And Other Prophetic Errors

Today, Witnesses are taught that the year 1914 marked the "presence" of Jesus, which is their version of his Second Coming. The year also marked the "end of the Gentile times." Witnesses state that the turmoil occurring on earth in 1914 was fulfillment of Scripture. The 1978 booklet called *Jehovah's Witnesses in the Twentieth Century* says (p. 7) regarding 1914: "Not all that was expected to happen in 1914 did happen." By now, we can properly wonder just what they had expected. By their statement, it sounds as though they may have erred on a few small points. But we have learned that their editorial policy is used to subtly modify or change previous error or previous interpretation. One "small" item they expected in 1914 was the *end of the world!*

In Russell's *Thy Kingdom Come* (p. 23) we read the following: "The time of the end, a period of 115 years, from A.D. 1799 to 1914, is particularly marked in the Scriptures." In his *Time Is at Hand* (p. 101):

> Be not surprised, then, when in subsequent chapters we present proof that the setting up of the kingdom of God has already begun, that it is pointed out in prophecy as due to begin the exercise of power in A.D. 1878, and that the battle of the great day of God Almighty of Rev. 16:14 which will end in A.D. 1914 with the complete overthrow of earth's present rulership is already commenced.

Read this carefully. The 1915 edition of this book changed the text to read from A.D. 1914 as quoted above to read A.D. 1915;

37

otherwise the statement is exactly the same. It simply was moved up a year with no explanation.

In the *Watchtower,* July 15, 1894:

> The old is quickly passing and the new is coming in. Now, in view of recent labor troubles and threatened anarchy, our readers are writing to know if there may not be a mistake on their 1914 date. They say that they do not see how present conditions can hold out so long under the strain. We see no reason for changing the figures—nor could we change them if we would. They are, we believe, God's dates, not ours. But bear in mind that the end of 1914 is not the date for the *beginning,* but for the *end* of the time of trouble.

It is most clear the teaching was at that time that the government and powers on earth would be destroyed and overcome in the battle of Armageddon of October, 1914. So "not all that was expected to happen did happen." It sure didn't.

A second erroneous prophecy exists about 1914. Since Jesus did not physically come for A. H. MacMillan and other Witness leaders in Bethel Headquarters in 1914, this created a temporary dilemma, but Russell was told by an Adventist preacher that the Greek word used in Scripture for "coming" could also mean "presence." The use of this meaning would allow them to declare that Jesus actually did come as prophesied since they could explain that this "presence" constituted the expected coming!

In time, Russell and then Rutherford still clung to the year 1914 as fulfillment of prophecy (just as they had expected, they said) but now the meaning had changed. Rather than the end of the world as they said, Russell called their attention to the fact it was not the beginning of the end but that October 1914 would see the *end* of the *end.* But now, rather than the end, Armageddon, 1914, became the beginning of the end. So this version says now that the Gentile times ended in 1914 and Jesus came by not coming but by turning his attention (from up in heaven) toward the earth. This, they say, constitutes a coming. So, since he didn't really come back to earth, his "visible organization" on earth was still needed, and the faithful slave would need to continue to give out spiritual food. But Christ's nonreturn caused problems in the organization.

Russell's death in 1916 was almost the last straw. Rutherford took over and began to reorganize. The ensuing battle, Rutherford said, fulfilled more Scriptures, and so Rutherford declared in 1918 Jesus "returned to the temple," which is explained to mean that the organization was cleansed of the opposers (*Preparation*, 1933).

Around 1920 Rutherford decided he had found the new date for Armageddon—1925! He delivered a lecture that stirred up a lot of people; it was entitled "Millions Now Living Will Never Die." The speech was put in booklet form in 1920 and widely distributed. His opening statement said that although many would call it presumptuous, the reasonable conclusion was that millions now living on earth in 1920 would never die. Rutherford developed the theme in the book that the World War of 1914 was a great and final war spoken of by Jesus in Matthew 24. Next, Rutherford explained that the end times continued (remember, it is now 1920). He said there was presently famine, pestilence, Spanish flu, and earthquakes, which he said actually meant revolutions.

The next fulfillment cited was that God's favor returned to the Jewish nation exactly on time in 1878. He cites proof of this on page 78. The book says that God never intended that the Jews be destroyed and that they never shall be (pp. 28-38). Much attention, in fact, is given to the Jewish state. Zionism, he said, was destined to succeed. As of February 16, 1920, the Jews were returning to Israel. Houses were being built in preparation for the constant flow of Jews returning to the homeland. (The above about the Jews and Israel is denied in its entirety by present-day Witnesses who have been taught that they themselves are spiritual Israel and that God has abandoned the physical Jewish nation.)

Rutherford offered other signs of proof that 1925 was *the* year. Attacks were made on the clergy (he said that everyone knows there are two classes of ministers—good and bad), Wall Street, Catholics, Protestants. So the end was less than five years away. On page 88 Rutherford explained how he arrived at the year 1925. (Copies of the book are still available for those who would check this out, although you can't, of course, get them from the Watchtower Society.) Suffice to say that he was very wrong again. But he was not just wrong. He was really *wrong*. *He also prophesied that Abraham, Isaac, Jacob and others would be resurrected on earth to become God's earthly rulers:*

> . . . and since other Scriptures clearly fix the fact that there will be a resurrection of Abraham, Isaac, Jacob and other faithful ones of old, and that these will have the first favor, we may expect 1925 to witness the return of these faithful men of Israel from the condition of death, being resurrected and fully restored to perfect humanity, and made the visible, legal representatives of the new order of things on earth (p. 88).

Even with the two major failures and all the minor failures, it was still years before the society caught on about fixing dates. In the book *Life* (1929), it was said that the end was very close because the Jews were returning to Palestine. Soon after this, a new interpretation about Israel came forth. When Rutherford died in 1942, he was living in a house that had been built for Abraham and the others called Beth Sarim.

The following are of note:

Salvation (1939, p. 310): The disasters of Armageddon are just ahead.

Religion (1940, p. 338): The day for final settlement is at hand.

Children (1941): A story of two young people who are instructed to wait until after Armageddon to get married because the time is too short.

A New World Is at the Doors (1942): No comment needed here.

The Truth Shall Make You Free (1943): The end is dangerously near.

The Kingdom Is at Hand (1944, p. 342): The end of the world arrangement is now near.

Let God Be True (1946, p. 194): The disaster of Armageddon greater than that which befell Sodom and Gomorrah is at the door. This means Everlasting Life. It is unavoidable for Jehovah's time has come.

Watchtower (August 15, 1968): "Why Are You Looking Forward to 1975?" Readers might venture a guess as to the subject of this article. If they keep at it, one day they will get it right. But Jesus said none of us knows when that day will come.

These errors serve to demonstrate that "no one" includes the Watchtower Society. So they will know when we all know. The Witnesses still cling to the year 1914 as important in prophecy in world history. Early books contain page after page and quote after quote in regard to their view of the significance of that year. But their literature of today appears to be placing different emphasis on 1914 and calling less attention to it. At first, this year would be the end of the world, the end of the Gentile times and the time of Christ's return. Then 1914 became the end of the Gentile times, the onset of Jesus' presence and the beginning of the end of the world, which would be completed within one generation. As time since 1914 nears the third generation, it is quite obvious that this keystone in Witness dogma is crumbling, so at this point all they have left for the year 1914 is the end of the Gentile times (whatever they mean by that).

Dishonest Journalism

Dedicated followers of the Watchtower Society will not consider the possibility of dishonesty in any form charged to the organization or their leaders in Brooklyn. They will allow the possibility of some mistakes by local leaders, including such things as adultery or denying their gospel, which they call the Truth, because they have witnessed such in their own congregation. But Witnesses defend with intensity the leaders in Brooklyn, although they hardly know them, have never seen many of them, and know nothing of their personal background.

Some ex-Witnesses and others have written books and letters to members, friends, and relatives concerning various disagreements with the Watchtower organization. But the Witnesses have been told that these are members of the evil slave class and therefore should not be listened to or associated with, nor, of course, should their books be read. This makes it tough for a Witness to find out for himself or herself whether there is any basis for allegations made against the organization. An interesting situation is recognized. They won't even investigate.

Nevertheless, there are many outstanding examples to show that the Watchtower Society has used dishonest and deceptive journalism. Michael Van Buskirk in his book, *The Scholastic Dishonesty of the Watchtower,* presents absolute, positive proof of the tactics used by the Watchtower Society. In the face of such undeniable evidence, one wonders how such deception is used without fear of exposure. Then we remember that Witnesses, followers of the Watchtower Society, feel that all things published or stated by Brooklyn are straight from God, so their minds don't deal with possible error, and they are preconditioned toward error. They have been told just how to react to things that might seem like error. As one Witness said when asked about a change from the use of B.C. and A.D. terminology, she said, "I wondered about that and still don't understand why, but we had a talk on it and they explained it." So, although she still did not understand the explanation, she felt that since it was explained, it was okay and that she just didn't understand.

But Buskirk presents photocopies and direct quotes. The following examples demonstrate the incredible liberties taken by the Watchtower Society even to the point of partially, falsely, or treacherously quoting known scholars who are not Jehovah's Witnesses.

A Manual of Grammar of the Greek New Testament, the highly respected text by Dana and Mantey, is cited in support of the Watchtower Society's New World translation of John 1:1, and this reference of support is found in Watchtower literature. When Buskirk asked Dr. Mantey if he did in fact support the society's position, Dr. Mantey replied, "My interpretation of John 1:1 in that same paragraph was 'the Word was Deity.' That is, that Christ is of the same essence as the Father, of the same family. So I was quoted out of context."

Is that honest scholarship? Dr. Mantey went on to say that they not only quoted him out of context, but that he was not even talking about what they quoted him as affirming. Dr. Mantey also wrote to the Watchtower Society, and Buskirk includes a copy of the letter in his book. In the letter, Dr. Mantey took strong exception to their quoting him. He took advantage of the opportunity to challenge the New World translation. He demanded that they not quote him again in their literature. A personal interview with Dr. Mantey is on cassette tape and is available to anyone from a group called CARIS (see appendix for address).

Buskirk's book also goes into much more detail on the subject as well as other major points of doctrine. This book is available and recommended to all and is listed in the appendix.

But our purpose here is to show the dishonest tactics employed by the society. Buskirk wrote to the society and their reply is included in his book. The book also settles for certain the issue of the faithful and discreet slave. He presents documented proof that Russell was at first the slave. Photostats of the Witnesses' own literature make this unmistakable in many quotations. We will extract only two short quotes here. From photostat no. 9:

> All the feet members who are now engaged in proclaiming this precious message received their enlightenment by partaking of the food which the Lord sent through his chosen servant. The Watchtower unhesitatingly proclaims Brother Russell as that faithful and wise servant.

From photostat no. 13: "Clearly, then, the Lord foretold an office that would be filled by a man."

Buskirk's book is highly recommended for any doubting Jehovah's Witness; the authenticity of the materials cannot be denied. No Jehovah's Witness could read this book of forty-eight pages without having his eyes opened. One point is undeniable. Until Rutherford changed the slave to a class, Russell was the slave.

An interesting sidelight is seen in Buskirk's book. Photostat no. 8 contains a portion of an article entitled "Brother Russell's Christmastide Greeting." The article explains that before he died, Russell gave instructions for the publication of a beautiful little card conveying his greetings and best wishes. On the back of the card was to be the famous painting of Christ stilling the storm on the sea. Since the Witnesses do not celebrate Christmas, the reader may decide for himself this activity of December 1916, and what meaning to apply to it.

MORE DECEPTION

"Not all that was expected to happen, happened" (*Jehovah's Witnesses in the Twentieth Century;* an article concerning 1914). Any Witness over forty years old knows what was expected. Could this major error be dismissed so lightly?

"Why are you looking forward to 1975?" (*Watchtower*, August 15, 1968, p. 494). Once again we could say that not all that was expected to happen, happened.

On the witness stand in court in 1974, Watchtower vice-president and legal counsel Hayden Covington (who apparently has since left the Watchtower) admitted that the society promulgated false prophecy to fulfill an erroneous statement. For the sake of unity, although false, the prophecy must be accepted by all Jehovah's Witnesses and failure to accept would lead to disfellowship. This was done in the Scottish court of sessions as quoted in a book by Edmund Gruss on the prophetic speculation of Jehovah's Witnesses and is referenced in the appendix.

More proof of the dishonesty of *Watchtower* statements about Jesus Christ follows:

> He was more than human . . . it seems clear that his divinity was retained in humanity because he repeatedly spoke of himself as having come down from heaven and because he, though passing through trial and sorrow as a man, was yet possessed of the authority and exercised the prerogatives of a God. He was the object of unreproved worship . . . (*Watchtower*, October, 1880).

It is evident from their own words that the *Watchtower* article did not consider Jesus just a perfect man. The above quote says that he was yet possessed of the authority and exercised the prerogatives of God.

The following quotes from Watchtower Society literature present the most devastating proof of dishonest journalism:

Article 2 of the Charter of Incorporation of the Watchtower Bible and Tract Society states: "The purposes of this Society are . . . public Christian worship of Almighty God and Jesus Christ; to arrange for and hold local and worldwide assemblies for such worship . . ." In the *1969 Yearbook of Jehovah's Witnesses,* the charter is quoted again. Notice how it is misquoted: "And for public Christian worship of Almighty God . . ."

It is obvious they have dubiously and dishonestly altered their own quotation, the purpose being to avoid the reference to worship of Jesus Christ. It is astounding that an organization claiming to be earth's only representative to Jehovah would resort to such dishonest tactics. But they quoted this same passage again in the 1971 *Watchtower* and again changed the direct quote.

One must be extremely gullible and close-minded to simply accept these evidences of dishonesty, but anyone willing to review society literature soon realizes that the tactics of distorting even their own literature is a common, constant practice. More proof is available; Edmond Gruss quotes numerous editions of the *Watchtower*. For example, "Yes, we believe our Lord while on earth was really worshipped and properly so" (*Watchtower,* July 15, 1898, p. 2337).

Those familiar with Watchtower Society teachings will note here that faced with these facts about their history, the society decided that when the word meaning worship was used in relation to Jesus, it meant "do obeisance" rather than "worship." Of course, the only support for this is found in society literature. Other times, the society will take the position that, yes, we worship Jesus, but it is not the same worship as Jehovah. More play on words.

Witnesses all agree today that Jesus' Second Coming was really his presence, and he has already come by turning his attention toward the earth. The Witnesses presently believe, therefore, that Jesus will not come again as is commonly believed by most all Christians. The Witness book *Make Sure of All Things* (1965, p. 431) states that Christ's return is not a literal coming back to earth. *Watchtower* book *Let God Be True* (1952, chapter 17) describes their view of Christ's return. It warns not to expect a visible return and states that Christ already is present; therefore, he has already come.

Now, if you aren't yet sufficiently confused, read these quotes: On Our Lord's return, "And he shall send Jesus Christ . . . whom the heaven must retain until the times of restitution . . ."; "He certainly referred to a second personal coming"; "the time of his appearing" (*Studies in the Scriptures,* 1886, vol. 1, chapter 6).

The Watchtower Society set the time of Jesus' second presence at various dates. Among them was 1874 and their most popular date has been 1914. Whichever, the claim is made that Jesus is already, since that date, present, so if he is already present, then we no longer need to look for his coming. But Watchtower literature, although insisting that Jesus already came, or is present, is beginning to take a new twist. Believe it or not, Witnesses, your publications once again are looking for Jesus' return.

For example, in the Witness book *The Truth Shall Make You Free* (1941) chapter 23, entitled "Manner of the King's Coming," explains in much detail that Jesus returned although invisibly in 1914 (p. 293). Written forty years ago, this book continued to publish and declare the Russell theory that thirty-one years before 1941, Jesus "came." Those who have been Jehovah's Witnesses during many of these years know without hesitation that this has been taught. In fact, their literature abounds with this theology. But nearly seventy years have passed since the 1914 prediction. Are the Brooklyn editors about to bury this coming only to replace it by another later one?

"The Year 1914, a Turning Point in Human History" (*Jehovah's Witnesses in the Twentieth Century,* article, page 7). The article quoted explains the Witness view of the great importance of the year 1914, but it does not mention the return of Christ. Surely we could not conclude that his return was not important enough to be pointed out in the article. Why was this important event not stated prominently in this recent 1978 article?

If we read *Choosing the Best Way of Life* (1979, p. 36), we see that Christ's coming in glory is sure: "The certainty of Christ's coming"; "Confirm to them that Jesus' coming in kingdom power would indeed be glorious"; "Faith in Jesus' arrival in kingdom power"; "The transfiguration also served to establish the certainty of Jesus' coming and power." Especially note these quotes: "Until that grand day when the day star, the Lord Jesus Christ reveals himself in all his magnificent glory"; "The revelation of the Son of God *will* spell [not *did* spell] destruction for the faithless ones."

Honest evaluation of these statements makes it plain that they are done in future tense and future inference. Nowhere in this article do we find that Jesus' return was in the year 1914, and nowhere in the article is it made clear that his coming is really a presence. Far from it. We can well wonder just what is the society telling its followers in the 1980s? Do these quotes indicate a presence since 1914? Or do they represent a hedge between the previous teaching of the presence and something they're building up to?

On page 176, "The revelation of the Lord Jesus Christ will then not be a time . . ." Notice that the future tense is used. On page 175, "Unexpectedly as when a thief comes, the Lord Jesus Christ will be revealed." This quote tells us that at his coming, his revealing will be unexpected as a thief. This certainly can't apply to something we've known about since the year 1914. A quote from page 175, "Because of such revelation, the Lord Jesus Christ can come at any time," speaks for itself. If the reader at this point is still not convinced, how could we possibly misunderstand the intent of this quote from page 185, "In fact, our recognizing that the Lord Jesus Christ could come at any time . . ."

Reader, what do you think this means? We will add only two more quotes to this part. In the Witness book *The Truth That Leads to Eternal Life* (1968) chapter 10 is entitled, "God's Kingdom Comes to Power in the Midst of Its Enemies." In paragraph 5: "That event has already taken place in the heavens. Kingdom authority has already been given to Jehovah's son." Does that sound strange to you? "God's only organization" discovered that Christ came in 1914, and they boldly proclaimed this in many publications and on the platforms for more than seventy years. Is it more than interesting to notice how they deal with this subject today?

We encourage Witnesses to check this out in their own

Watchtower literature. If it could be said in straightforward language for seventy years that Jesus has been present since 1914, what conclusions can we reach from the literature that now makes no reference to 1914? Why continually use the words "come," "coming," "arrival," etc.? Is it deceptive to use those terms if you really believe that he's not coming, that he won't arrive, that he has already come? Only one very obvious conclusion can be drawn—this is dishonest journalism. But the provable fact is that dishonest journalism, evasive techniques, and frank changes have long existed in Witness publications. There are more examples. In Russell's *Thy Kingdom Come* (1907), "And the full establishment of the kingdom of God in the earth at A.D. 1914" (p. 126). This same book, published by the same people in the 1925 edition, on the same page offers the same quotation as, "And the full establishment of the kingdom of God in the earth after 1914." Notice the change? The 1907 edition said "at A.D. 1914," and the 1925 edition said "after 1914."

In the 1901 edition of the same book, on page 324, "Thus, the pyramid witnesses that the close of 1874 was a chronological beginning of the time of trouble." In the 1907 edition the same quote offers, "Thus, the pyramid witnesses that the close of 1914 would be the beginning of the time of trouble." Notice the change? These examples are from the same book in various editions, and they were taken from actual photocopies of the original pages. There are more examples. Professor Edmond Gruss did considerable study and presents much more living proof; he is referenced in the appendix.

DISHONESTY BY USE OF ELLIPSIS

In English grammar, the ellipsis (. . .) is often used in order to quote the more important portions of a statement, while not including those that are secondary. However, the ellipsis should not be used in such manner as to make a statement appear to say something different from what is actually stated. Everyone will agree that such misuse of the ellipsis is deceptive and dishonest. We will examine its use by the Watchtower Society.

The treatment by use of ellipsis in quoting the charter of the Watchtower, Article 2, is shown earlier in this chapter. It is mentioned here again to call attention to their use of the ellipsis in a deceptive way. The Witnesses of the year 1969 were told not to worship Jesus. Hence, the Watchtower "simply left these words out" without explanation. Here is a striking example of deceptive use of the ellipsis. In the *Watchtower* of May 15, 1977, in a question from the readers on page 319, the reader had asked that John 1:1 be explained. Part of the explanation quoted William Barclay, whom the Watchtower Society called a noted Bible translator. Read this carefully. They quote Barclay: "The word was in the same class as God, belonged to the same order of being as God . . . [notice the placement of the ellipsis here by the *Watchtower* editors] John is not here identifying the Word with God. To put it very simply, he does not say that Jesus was God." Their quotation is taken from the book by William Barclay entitled *Many Witnesses, One Lord* (pp. 23, 24). What did the ellipsis leave out? What did Barclay say that the Witnesses did not quote? The next statement by Barclay in his book and omitted by the Watchtower by ellipsis said: "The only modern translator who fairly and squarely faces this problem is Kenneth West, who has, 'The word was as to his essence essential deity.' But it is here that the New English Bible, or the N.E.B., has brilliantly solved the problem with the absolutely accurate rendering: 'what God was, the Word was.' "

The last sentence by Barclay quoted by the Watchtower was, "To put it very simply, he does not say that Jesus was God." But the next line in Barclay's book, which they did not quote, says, "What he does say is that no human description of Jesus can be adequate in that Jesus, however you're going to define it, must be described in terms of God."

The crux of the episode of Barclay's quote is seen in Barclay's own words to Dr. Donald Shumaker of Biola College. Barclay said:

> The *Watchtower* article has, by judicious cutting, made me say the opposite of what I meant to say. What I was meaning to say, as you well know, is that Jesus is not the same as

God; to put it more crudely that he is of the same stuff as God, that is of the same being as God, but the way the *Watchtower* has printed my stuff, has simply left the conclusion that Jesus is not God in a way that suits themselves. If they've missed from their answer, the translation of Kenneth West and the N.E.B., they missed the whole point.

For those who will see, this chapter provides ample proof of deceptive, dishonest journalism employed by the Watchtower Society. For those who would still doubt, the materials presented here should provide a good starting point for further investigation.

It is a serious thing to accuse an organization that claims to be God's organization, in fact, God's only organization. The Watchtower Society claims to be the spokesman for God, delivering "meat in due season" and claiming further that outside this organization there is no contact with God. This means (if one believes it to be true) that *one must find his way to God as a member of the organization!* Now, you may be doubtful or amazed, even, that this could be true. Does the Watchtower Society really claim this? Do the followers of the society really believe there is no other way to contact God? *Yes, they do.* Let us examine the lead article in a recent *Watchtower* (March 1, 1979). The title of the article is "Put Faith in a Victorious Organization." From the title alone, it is clear that the attention is directed toward faith in an organization. It did not say put faith in God. Here are some claims made in the article:

1. This organization of God first appeared in 1513 B.C.E. with the founding of the twelve Jewish tribes.
2. "Theocratic organization" importance is stressed, getting equal billing with God.
3. No one in all the universe loves the theocratic organization more than Jesus Christ. So he was put to death because of unswerving devotion to the theocratic organization. (Some people think he gave his life for a different reason.)
4. God pulled away from the Jews because they rejected the

theocratic organization, but the few who did not reject it were placed in a new theocratic organization at Pentecost.

5. So the organization changed from Jewish to Christian. Now they constituted one visible theocratic organization.

6. Read number 1 again. The organization became 'visible *twice* for the *first* time?

7. Then the article moved over the centuries. It claimed that Christendom's confusion became dizzying so a small group decided to pull away. They earnestly sought to become Jehovah's visible organization and instrument. Evidently this is all they needed to do for God to declare them His only organization.

Obviously since this is God's organization the above can be substantiated in the Bible. Well, the average Witness doesn't know whether it can or not, because the average Witness does not even check the information he is given. It takes an imaginative mind to produce such a story as presented here (which, by the way, has changed from earlier stories of their origin). Try to substantiate it with Scripture. You really do need faith in this organization, and lots of it, to believe this sort of thing.

7

When Members Leave the Society

When people leave the society who have been Witnesses long enough to be fully indoctrinated, they find the path very difficult for a time, and for some a long time, after they learn the real truth. They are angry or frustrated to discover mistruths, and many hang on or even keep on attending meetings even though they have discovered that much is wrong. Some continue to attend the meetings for a long time, not sharing their new feelings with any of the local members. Some disassociate themselves from all religions. Many become atheists; most go through varying degrees of anguish. The skeptical attitude they have been taught toward all the world—including religion, education, politics, business—becomes a real stumbling block for them. One person suffered severe headaches and episodes of acute tension and hypertension requiring medical care.

Some ex-Witnesses have described their ordeal. One such was William J. Schnell. In his two books, *Thirty Years a Watchtower Slave* and *Jehovah's Witnesses Errors Exposed,* Schnell told of the pressures upon him. He had been very deep into the organization, spending four years at Bethel (the Brooklyn headquarters) and twenty-one years in full-time Witness activity. (He placed over 200,000 Witness books.) Schnell's parents had been Witnesses, and he relates how his father, on his deathbed, confessed to him that he had no assurance of salvation. Just before he died, Schnell's father repented and found peace. He asked his son to tell the story over his grave, but instead a man from Bethel gave the talk, and no reference was made to Schnell's father's repentance. At that time, Schnell was still a devout Witness, but he does relate to being very shocked and confused at his father's deathbed conversion.

Schnell stated that upon looking back, he recognized seven areas of doubt that began to press him. First, he knew Jesus Christ died on the cross for all our sins, yet he knew he was pressing people to work harder and harder to gain salvation at Armageddon. Second, he knew that Scripture taught that we were all lost and must come to Christ—yet he was teaching that refuge and safety were available only within the Watchtower Society. Third, he began to wonder just how scriptural was the practice of hours of service placing books and obeying the society. Fourth, instead of finding the peace and rest promised by Jesus, Schnell, even after thirty years, felt no such peace. Fifth, over the years, he watched their doctrine change 148 times between 1917 and 1928. Sixth, in the Book of Acts, Schnell read that Jesus tells us to become His witnesses. Yet he knew that he was a "Jehovah's Witness," and he also knew that he received that name from a man, Rutherford. And seventh, Schnell could not understand why even after working diligently all those years to achieve salvation, he knew he still had no assurance of it.

Another ex-Witness, who had been at headquarters as house-keeper, told of the way several were humiliated in the dining hall by President Knorr. She also commented on the well-publicized fact that all the Bethelites, including Knorr, received room and board and fourteen dollars a month. Yet, President Knorr lived in a penthouse apartment on the tenth floor. His apartment was decorated with murals. He had a private kitchen, television, and personal cook. He traveled in a Cadillac and took people to expensive restaurants and Broadway shows. She commented that people donated to Knorr personally, and he used his expense account to travel first class. This ex-Witness resigned from Bethel in 1958 and married a man who also had been at Bethel. After a conflict regarding blood transfusions, her husband was expelled from the Watchtower Society, and, because she supported her husband's position, she too was disfellowshipped. In the book, *We Left Jehovah's Witnesses,* by Edmond Gruss, she explains the considerable problems which developed because her Witness parents disowned her. Her husband's story is also given in this book. More on this couple later.

8

The Lord's Supper: The Witnesses Celebrate It Differently

Jesus told His followers to "keep doing this in remembrance of me" as He shared the Last Supper with them. So, Jesus' followers down to this time have done as Christ instructed. Scripture and historical evidence show that the early church followed this admonition, at one point being scolded by Paul (Corinthians) because they had not properly and honorably conducted the ceremony. Christ's church continues to observe this ordinance to this day. But for Jehovah's Witnesses only certain ones may "do this in remembrance." There is, of course, no scriptural support for the Witness doctrine that only certain ones—they say only the "remnant"—are allowed to partake of the emblems.

There is less support (if there could be less) for their requirement that although one cannot partake he or she should still attend the ceremony. In their annual celebration of this event today, almost no one in the congregation does participate. In this Witness version of Easter, where they have the largest number in attendance, a message is given explaining why they don't take the emblems. They are told that only members of the remnant, the "faithful servant class," the 144,000 (now down to 10,000) are worthy to partake. If one of these qualified ones happens to be at the service, he will participate. Otherwise, the emblems are passed among the audience after the "talk," and the service is over.

Witness literature claims that this is the scriptural procedure as followed by the early church (and only Witnesses do things like the early church did). Witnesses must not fall prey to the errors of "Christendom!"

Here again is an example of the society's twisting of Scripture, of connecting various verses of the Bible. There is no substantive scriptural support for this man-made doctrine. Think a moment about some of the "worthies" who participated at the original Lord's Supper! That very night they *all* ran away from Jesus, and Peter (the Rock) denied that he even *knew* Jesus. Would either of these qualify for remnant membership in the Jehovah's Witnesses?

There is historical proof describing the celebration by the early church. *Halley's Bible Handbook,* a respected publication for many years, quotes some of the writings of Justin Martyr, a Christian writer who lived in the years A.D. 100-167. Martyr was born about the time the Apostle John died. Martyr was said to be one of the most able of the early Christian church and of his time. Significant to our subject here, he described a typical worship service of the early congregation. He said that a weekly meeting was held of the Christians who "live in the cities and villages." Martyr described the activities of the meeting: "Then the consecrated elements are distributed to each one and partaken of, and are carried by the deacons to the houses of the absent." Any Jehovah's Witnesses should be interested in this description, which shows clearly that the elements were *distributed to each one and partaken of, even carried to the homes of the absent!*

This surely deserves deeper exploration. One method is to read all texts in the Bible on the subject for their true meaning, then evaluate the explanation of Scripture as expounded to you by others. When you come to realize the real truth, Witness friend, you will see that you are being deprived, by the society, of a *personal* experience with the Lord, established by Jesus Christ Himself. Will you check it out?

9

Disfellowshipping

"Disfellowshipping," or expelling a member from the society, is a serious act and one of the most feared swords hanging over the heads of Witnesses. It can have devastating effects, separating parents and children, husbands and wives, relatives and friends. Disfellowshipping has separated families to such an extent that a Witness will not even correspond by mail with disfellowshipped family members, even for the rest of their lives. A Witness parent must not welcome back into the home his own grown child who has been disfellowshipped nor so much as acknowledge him or her in the street. A person who has been disfellowshipped in effect is dead to all the other members of the society.

The Witness book entitled *Your Word Is a Lamp to My Feet* explains more about disfellowshipping. The congregation is not allowed to vote on disfellowshipping of a member; in fact, they are not even told what the "crime" is. Headquarters instructs that they need only say to the congregation that the person was guilty of "conduct unbecoming a Christian" and this is as far into it as they go. The actual decision of disfellowshipping is made by a committee composed of the chief minister, his assistant, and the Bible study servant. The above book says,

> When anyone is disfellowshipped . . . a resolution is drawn up by the judicial committee and presented to the congregation informing them that the individual has been disfellowshipped for conduct unbecoming a Christian. The congregation is not invited to vote on this resolution. The committee is responsible for acting on behalf of the entire

57

congregation because they have made the investigation. Those who love Jehovah's law and His righteousness will accept the decision making and not complain against those responsible for handling the matter (Num. 16:41-50; Ps. 119:29-30) (p. 179).

Of course, a member cannot believe anything contrary to the society, nor can he get ahead of the society, which some have done to their dismay:

Everyone that proceeds ahead and does not remain in this teaching of the Christ does not have God . . . If anyone comes to you and does not bring this teaching, neither receive him into your home or say a greeting to him for he that says a greeting to him is a sharer in his wicked works. In faithfulness to God, none in the congregation should greet such persons when meeting them in public nor should they welcome them into their home—even blood relatives who do not live in the same home . . . avoid contact with them just as much as possible. And those who may be members of the same household with a disfellowshipped person, cease sharing spiritual fellowship with the wrongdoer. If a disfellowshipped person attends a service, none will greet him, of course.

Now, parents, observe this quote from the book *Organization for Kingdom Preaching and Disciplemaking:*

This does not mean that parents would stop counseling or disciplining a baptized child who had been disfellowshipped and who was living in the same home with them . . . this, however, does not mean fellowshipping spiritually with the child in a regular study in which he is approved as an approved sharer to share in such family studies. The child would first have to show repentance and change and be reinstated by the Judicial Committee.

Parents, is any comment needed here? This means that you could not engage in Bible study, even *Watchtower* magazine study, until such time as the committee reinstated the child! And according to *Your Word Is a Lamp to My Feet,* this reinstatement requires a minimum period of one year or more (p. 181). Do you see any of the redeeming love of Christ in these proceedings? Perhaps you would agree with disfellowshipping procedures for murderers, adulterers and the like, especially for adults, but can you agree to such action that forbids a parent from studying the Bible or having a spiritual relationship with a son or daughter?

Here are some examples of disfellowshipping: William Cetnar tells his story in the book *We Left Jehovah's Witnesses, A Non-Prophet Organization* by Edmond Gruss. Mr. Cetnar had been a Witness since 1940. In 1947, at age 18, he began full-time Witness preaching and in 1950 was appointed to work at the Watchtower Society's headquarters called Bethel. He soon was assigned to work in the service department, which handled problems and answered letters. It also acted as a court of appeals in disfellowshipping cases. By 1958, and after years at the top and after considerable experiences (as related in the book mentioned and on a tape cassette available today in Christian bookstores), Cetnar began to have reservations. He left the headquarters and eventually became a Bible study servant in a congregation in Pennsylvania.

Cetnar describes the beginning of his disfellowshipping. It started when the grandparents of a young child whose doctor wanted to give him a blood transfusion asked Cetnar what he would do if it were his child. Cetnar told them he would let the doctor decide. This statement caused Cetnar to appear at a hearing, and he was later disfellowshipped.

A point of interest made by Cetnar is that in 1949 his wife's grandfather, who was a member of the remnant, *received* a blood transfusion, and her father, who was the presiding minister of the congregation at the time, and her uncle both gave blood. Cetnar commented that he himself personally had never given blood nor received a transfusion, but he was disfellowshipped because of the statement and recommendation he made to those grandparents.

In the same book, Cetnar's wife, Joan, tells how she also was disfellowshipped. She was born to parents who were staunch

Jehovah's Witnesses, and she grew up in that environment. Her parents were close friends of Nathan Knorr, Watchtower Society president, who was a regular visitor in her home. Joan was baptized in 1948 by her father. She also spent some years at Bethel, and she comments about life there. She related considerable information on the hierarchy of the society, and she describes her husband's disfellowshipping proceedings. He was not allowed any witnesses for his side. Afterward her father informed her husband that he (William) could not stay any longer with her parents where they were living on a farm owned by her father, so they moved to California. Her Witness sister-in-law had a blood transfusion given to her sick poodle. Cetnar told her the society would not approve and chided her jokingly into writing Brooklyn to find out. They replied that she had done wrong. The sister-in-law was very annoyed and amazed, and she commented that the cat never drained the blood of the mice. Later, Joan was disfellowshipped after she was reported for attending a talk that her husband gave on the Witnesses at a church. Afterward her parents wrote her off and would not answer her letters anymore.

Another ex-Witness relates the events of her disfellowshipping. She and her husband began to realize contradictions and failures in Witness doctrine. They gradually began to stay away from meetings and stopped going in 1962. Then, in 1968, she met a friend who was a Jehovah's Witness, and she shared her reasons for leaving the organization. A few weeks later, an overseer of the congregation came to see her to find out whether or not she would return to the Kingdom Hall. She was visited again the next Sunday, and a warning was given that action would be taken if she did not return. That's the last official thing she heard, but, subsequently, when she met another Witness friend she had known for years and tried to greet him, she was told, "I am not allowed to talk to you."

There is only one attitude allowed if you are a devoted Witness. You must meekly do as you are told. If you ask a question or challenge a doctrine, you'll be put under suspicion and warned to get back on the track. If you don't, they will write you off by disfellowshipping. By this act, the congregation is informed that you are out of step and must be put out of their lives. The organization is geared so that any opposing idea is immediately put down. Fear of disfellowshipping keeps many members who have developed doubts from investigating them any further. All food, all thought, all interpretation must come from Brooklyn. All they need you for is to follow orders. Disfellowshipping often separates families because some cannot agree with the food from Brooklyn. Try as you may, it is impossible to look upon these acts as acts of love. If God is love, would He not allow a parent to hold a Bible study with his child without waiting for the committee to give its okay? Would you wait for the committee to give its okay?

10

The Witnesses Write Their Own Bible

The Jehovah's Witnesses are the only religious group who have a Bible that exactly matches their doctrine. And well it should, because they wrote it. Throughout their earlier history, they have consulted and quoted many versions and translations of the Bible in their religious work. However, their own translation, done in the 1950s, is the one they now use. This is the version they keep in their homes and take to meetings, and this is the version they use to prove doctrine.

Just how did it come into being and when? Do they have scholars capable of such work? One thing is sure, the average Witness does not know how his Bible came to be, who translated it, or how good or dependable the translation is. In this instance, as in everything else, the Witnesses just accept it. They don't investigate anything. They don't submit their Bible to scholars, nor do they make any personal effort to check its accuracy.

The same cannot be said about all the other translations. In their view, all others, in one way or another, fall short. The only one they totally accept is the one they were told to accept. Their Bible is called the New World Translation. Even their governing body simply accepts it.

Marley Cole, in his pro-Witness book, *Jehovah's Witnesses,* explains how the president of the society continued to exercise unrestricted power over the organization by describing how this Bible was introduced (p. 88). Cole quotes the *Watchtower* of Sept. 15, 1950, using the release of this Bible as an example of the way the president exercised unrestricted freedom. The *Watch-tower* says that on September 3, 1949, President Knorr convened a joint meeting of the boards of both their corporations and announced to the directors the existence of a "New World Bible Translation Committee" and that the committee had completed a translation of the Christian Greek Scriptures. Obviously, the board of directors had not known that such work was officially in progress, nevertheless completed. Knorr said that the committee, which in reality consisted of himself and a few others, had on the day just before the meeting turned over the translation to the society, and he accepted it for the society.

This is how the directors investigated and accepted. Knorr said that he himself had read the entire translation, and, upon request, he read several chapters to "let the directors see the nature of the translation." Favorable comments ensued, and it was moved, accepted, and adopted that the society accept this "gift." How simply amazing! Ex-Witness William Cetnar was working at the headquarters when the translation work was done. Although the names of the committee members were and are kept secret, their identity was common knowledge at Bethel, according to Cetnar. He named Knorr and four others as the translators. None of these had adequate background for the job. Knorr was a high school graduate. One member, F. W. Franz, who was the society vice-president, did have some language training. However, in a court trial in Scotland, Franz was asked to translate the fourth verse of Genesis, chapter two, in Hebrew, and his answer was he could not.

The New World Translation was released in volumes until full Old and New Testaments were produced in one volume. Early editions used footnotes, which were eliminated in later editions. Millions of copies have been printed and distributed. Their Bible is repeatedly updated with changes in wording, phrasing, and meaning constantly being done as the Witnesses receive "new light." Not unexpectedly, this translation supports the organization and its doctrine much much more than any other version. When necessary to make something more clear (that is, in agreement with the doctrine written before the translation was done), the translators have added words, changed words, left out words, and used brackets freely.

A group in Canada called the Help Jesus Ministry has compiled a list of comments regarding the New World Translation that were made by a worldwide cross section of Greek scholars.

Dr. J. R. Mantey, co-author of the popular Dana and Mantey *Greek Grammar,* states: "A shocking mistranslation . . . Obsolete and incorrect."

Dr. Bruce M. Metzger, professor of New Testament Language and Literature at Princeton University, states: "A frightful mistranslation."

Dr. Samuel J. Micolasi, Zurich, Switzerland, states: "It is monstrous to translate the phrase 'The Word was a god.' "

Dr. William Barclay, University of Glasgow, Scotland, and a leading Greek scholar, states: "The deliberate distortion of truth by this sect is seen in their New World Translation. John 1:1 is translated . . . the word was a god . . . , a translation which is grammatically impossible . . . it is abundantly clear that a sect which can translate the New Testament like this is intellectually dishonest."

Some of the most glaring faults in the New World Translation should be presented here for demonstration lest some reader feel that the scholars simply have a prejudice against Jehovah's Witnesses. A striking example is found in their rendering of Colossians 1:16-17. Witness readers may want to investigate this, using their Kingdom Interlinear Bible, which is their own publication. A major doctrine of the Witnesses is that Jesus was created by Jehovah. They say that Jesus was the very first creation of Jehovah. In the accepted translations, these two verses explain that in Jesus all things were created. The highly accepted American Standard Version says,

> For in Him all things were created, both in the heavens and on earth, visible and invisible, whether thrones or dominions, or rulers or authorities—all things have been created through Him and by Him, and He is before all things and in Him all things hold together.

Now, notice very carefully the subtle change in the language of the New World Translation:

> Because by means of Him all [other] things were created in the heavens and upon the earth, the things visible and the things invisible, no matter whether they are thrones or lordships or governments or authorities. All [other] things have been created through Him and for Him, also He is before all [other] things and by means of Him all [other] things were made to exist.

Did you notice? Read the two versions again. What is different? Yes, the word "other," inserted four times, is *not* in the Greek, *not in even their own Greek Bible,* the Kingdom Interlinear Translation. This is very serious business. By what possible authority could these so-called translators take such liberty? On page 6 of the foreword in the leatherbound version being used here (1961 edition) on the bottom of the page we find this short phrase, "Brackets enclose words inserted to complete the sense in English text." It takes no scholar at all to recognize that the bracketed word "other" as used here does not complete the sentence, but rather changes the sense. There's nothing in the Greek, nothing in the meaning expressed, nothing at all to support the use of the word "other," and they prove it themselves in their own literature. There can only be one reason for this action in their version. The *doctrine* of the translators established before the translation was done is the only possible support for their altering meaning. It must be believed here that most Witnesses do not know of this deliberate alteration of the book they cherish so much. That is the reason for selecting this obvious, glaring example which is so very easy to investigate. Witness reader, don't turn away. If only for your own justification, investigate the above verse. There are other places where new words were added. (See Phil. 2:9; Acts 10:36.)

The most famous, or infamous, verse is found in John 1:1, where the Witness Bible calls Jesus "a god," although the article "a" is not present in the Greek. Most Witnesses know about the modification of this verse. It is highly promoted and explained in much of their literature. It's explained as though they have made a discovery unknown to everyone else or in error by everyone else. Interestingly enough, the reason for the interpretation is based on grammatical construction of the Greek—supposedly. However, the New World Translation is in disagreement with all scholars; in fact, even the two translations they cite in support, *The Complete Bible, An American Translation* and *A New Translation of The Bible,* by James Moffitt, do not use the phrase "a god." Do you understand what the Witness Bible says in John 1:1? The inference is that Jehovah is the God, the only God. Yet Jesus, the Son of God, is a god, not the god, but in some way a god. And "not a god" is actually "just a god." A big God and a little god. This makes an otherwise understandable portion of Scripture complicated and misunderstood. Their rendering unmistakably presents for us two Gods. Yet, they themselves know there are not two Gods.

To further support their translation of John 1:1, the society *partially* quotes recognized authorities. One such is Dr. A. T. Robertson, the renowned Greek scholar. Yet, Dr. Robertson, in his book *Word Pictures in the New Testament,* vol. 5, says, "Undoubtedly here Jesus claims eternal existence with the absolute phrase used of God" (pp. 158-59). Another scholar quoted by the Witnesses is Dr. Julius R. Mantey, who, incidentally, was a student under Dr. Robertson. Dr. Mantey emphatically states that the Witnesses *misquoted* him. In a letter to the *Watchtower,* Mantey called attention to the misquote and requested that they not quote him or his works again. He further asked for a public apology in the *Watchtower* magazine, which, of course, was not done. For more detail regarding these scholars, plus photostats of letters to and from the society and an extensive interview with Dr. Mantey, see *The Scholastic Dishonesty of the Watchtower,* by Michael Van Buskirk, listed in the appendix of this book.

For the totally dedicated Witness, who looks neither to the right nor to the left, the New World Translation is *the one.* Any translation not in agreement with the New World Translation is simply, without consideration, wrong. Witnesses accept the New World Bible just like their directors accepted it—without question.

Even so, even with their own translation, the society does not want its followers to read the Bible without also reading the Bible aids. This admonition is also given as seen in the *Watchtower*, March 18, 1974 (p. 181). After a warning not to listen to radio and TV evangelists and to avoid outside Christian literature, a caution about Bible reading is given in paragraph sixteen: "While the Bible encourages practical study as a method of gaining accurate knowledge, it also says, 'one isolating himself will seek his own selfish longing against all practical wisdom, he will break forth.' Prov. 18:1. So we must seek out the association of others who, like ourselves, are anxious to know accurately the will of God." It is really immaterial that the quoted proverb did not refer to the reading of the Bible. The society doesn't allow God's Spirit to reveal Bible truths. That's the job of the Brooklyn office.

11

Blood Transfusions

One of the most widely known tenets of Witness doctrine is its stand against blood transfusions. Witnesses will submit to all forms of surgery, therapy, and drugs but will not give or receive a blood transfusion. Looking into their history, it is interesting that neither Russell nor Rutherford mentioned this or any other sanctions regarding medical care. The limitation apparently was placed on the Witnesses in July, 1945. In a *Watchtower* article entitled "The Sanctity of Blood," dated July 1, 1945, admonition was given that it was a violation of Scripture to transfuse blood.

According to the *World Book Encyclopedia,* blood transfusions were given before 1900, and the procedure became large scale after the beginning of blood typing in the early 1900s. Isn't it odd that the organization was fifty years old before the revelation was given? Witnesses received blood transfusions during these years. Must it be said that they are excused from the law? If a transfusion violates a very sacred ordinance, how could God's organization receive it so late and, therefore, not offer protection for the earlier members who violated it? It is difficult to imagine that Holy God would hide such an important ordinance, if it should be so, for so long a time. Of course, transfusions were not known in the Levitical times.

The Bible, even the verses quoted by the Witnesses, if taken in proper context, clearly can be seen to explain that animals are given to man for food, provided the blood has been drained. The Bible declares that blood represented life. Animal blood, never human blood, was used in sin offerings. The procedure for this was clearly spelled out in Scripture. Jesus Christ offered the only human sacrifice, which was the perfect sacrifice, whereas animals were not by any stretch of the imagination perfect sacrifice. No blood sacrifice was required after Jesus' death and, of course, this continues today. The Witnesses quote Scripture for support of their position. They also quote the medical dangers of blood transfusions in support of their position. Genesis 9 instructed Noah that animals and plants are to be food, but the animals must have their blood drained. God also told Noah in this passage that man's blood should not be shed by another, saying: "Whoso sheddeth man's blood by man shall his blood be shed." This does not indicate man consuming man's blood but, rather, man killing man.

Walter R. Martin, in *Jehovah of the Watchtower* (see appendix) dealt in great detail with this matter. Scripture quoted by the Witnesses is examined (Gen. 9:3-6; Lev. 4:4-7, 13-18, 22-30; Exod. 24:3-8; Heb. 9:11-22; particularly Lev. 17). Martin also dealt with the fuller meaning of the context and included much historical information about the sacrificial ritual and modern information on transfusions as well. We will not repeat this here, but the reader is referred to Martin's book. We call your explicit attention to Leviticus 17. If one reads all sixteen verses, you better understand what is being said. It is obvious to all that the society has strained the meaning of "blood."

Most surely the Bible warned that no flesh shall be eaten unless the blood is first drained because blood represents life. We must honestly consider what is meant by the text and the context. Pilate said he was "innocent of the blood of this man." What did he mean? In Matt. 27:6, "Since it is the price of blood." What does that statement mean?

Under Hebrew law, when someone was killed, someone else would become the victim's blood avenger. What does that mean? The subject of blood in Hebrew law is very interesting. To fully understand, one should also study the ordinances and requirements of sacrifice. Stephen Olford, in his book *The Tabernacle, Camping with God,* provides considerable information on the subject (see appendix). At any rate, the instructions regarding blood very clearly discussed consuming, a process with which all are familiar. Transfusion procedures in no way can be considered such.

12

The Cop-out—Proverbs 4:18

The Watchtower Society employs Scripture to cover up all their erroneous predictions, prophecies, and doctrinal error. Proverbs 4:18 says, "But the path of the righteous is like the light of dawn that shines brighter and brighter until the full day." This passage contains a father's advice to his son. Verse fourteen warns not to enter the path of the wicked, and verses sixteen and seventeen explain the consequences of the evil path. In verse eighteen the path of the righteous is shown to, like the dawning of the day, get brighter and brighter as the full day appears. Verse nineteen contrasts the path of the wicked. Rather than bright like day, it is constantly dark like night. But the society selected verse eighteen of this total context and applied this to themselves. The meaning they attach to the verse, which is not only out of context but also devoid of its true meaning, is that as time passes, the society learns more and more. Their path is getting brighter and brighter. This they say allows for their prophetic error. In fact, they say their followers should appreciate being associated with a group who so humbly changes its position when they "get more light." Still they insist that, even so, they alone have the truth and they alone have contact with God. The problem is could this be the way prophecy is fulfilled? Is the changing understanding of a group of people one hundred years old a fulfilling of prophecy?

The Watchtower Society admits it is not inspired. New light comes when a prophecy fails. The society has invented a term called "present truth," which allows the society to change truth

71

72

as circumstance dictates. When the world did not end in 1914, the error was covered up by the statement "all that was expected to happen didn't." This does not appear to be so honest and humble but more like deception. The society does not want its followers to notice the real errors made, and it has made many. Is the society made of false prophets? The Witnesses define a prophet in their book *Aid to Bible Understanding*: "The three essentials for establishing the credentials of a true prophet as given through Moses were: a true prophet would speak in Jehovah's name, the things foretold would come to pass, and his prophesying must promote true worship being in harmony with God's revealed word and commandment" (p. 1,348).

The *Watchtower* magazine tells us that the society is indeed a prophet. In the April 1, 1972, issue (p. 197) the quote is that the prophet was not one man but was a body of men and women: "It was a small group of footstep followers of Jesus Christ known at that time as International Bible Students. Today they are known as Jehovah's Christian Witnesses." And now, lest anyone doubt, this quote from the *Watchtower* of July 1, 1973, "Consider too the fact that Jehovah's organization alone in all the earth is directed by God's holy spirit" (p. 402).

From the above statements and others made, the Watchtower Society claims clearly to be the prophet. The society has, in fact, prophesied dates for the end of the world many times over the years. The society qualifies as a prophet by saying that prophecy must come true, yet none of its prophecies has come true. The Watchman Fellowship of Columbus, Georgia, has prepared the following list of prophecies that never materialized:

ONE HUNDRED YEARS OF DIVINE DIRECTION

1889   "The 'battle of the great day of God Almighty' (Rev. 16:14), which will end in A.D. 1914 with the complete overthrow of earth's present rulership is already commenced." *The Time Is at Hand*, p. 101 (1908 edition)

1897   "Our Lord, the appointed King, is now present, since October 1874," *Studies in the Scriptures,* vol. 4, p. 621

1916   "The Bible chronology herein presented shows that the six great 1000 year days beginning with Adam are ended, and that the great 7th Day, the 1000 years of Christ's Reign, began in 1873." *The Time Is at Hand,* p. 2

1918   "Therefore we may confidently expect that 1925 will mark the return of Abraham, Isaac, Jacob and the faithful prophets of old, particularly those named by the Apostle in Hebrews 11, to the condition of human perfection." *Millions Now Living Will Never Die,* p. 89

1922   "The date 1925 is even more distinctly indicated by the Scriptures than 1914. *The Watchtower* (9/1/22), p. 262

1923   "Our thought is, that 1925 is definitely settled by the Scriptures. As to Noah, the Christian now has much more upon which to base his faith than Noah had upon which to base his faith in a coming deluge." *The Watchtower* (4/1/23), p. 106

1925   "The year 1925 is here. With great expectation Christians have looked forward to this year. Many have confidently expected that all members of the body of Christ will be changed to heavenly glory during this year. This may be accomplished. It may not be. In his own due time God will accomplish his purposes concerning his people. Christians should not be so deeply concerned about what may transpire this year." *The Watchtower* (1/1/25), p. 3

Sept. 1925   "It is to be expected that Satan will try to inject into the minds of the consecrated, the thought that 1925 should see an end to the work." *The Watchtower,* p. 262

1926   "Some anticipated that the work would end in 1925, but the Lord did not state so. The difficulty was that the friends inflated their imaginations beyond reason; and that when their imaginations burst asunder, they were inclined to throw away everything." *The Watchtower,* p. 232

1931 "There was a measure of disappointment on the part of Jehovah's faithful ones on earth concerning the years 1914, 1918, and 1925, which disappointment lasted for a time . . . and they also learned to quit fixing dates." *Vindication,* p. 338

1941 "Receiving the gift, the marching children clasped it to them, not a toy or plaything for idle pleasure, but the Lord's provided instrument for most effective work in the remaining months before Armageddon." *The Watchtower,* p. 288

1968 "True, there have been those in times past who predicted an 'end' to the world, even announcing a specific date. Yet nothing happened. The 'end' did not come. They were guilty of false prophesying. Why? What was missing? Missing from such people were God's truths and the evidence that He was using and guiding them." *Awake* (10/8/68) (See Luke 21:8) "Why Are You Looking Forward to 1975?" *The Watchtower* (8/15/68), p. 494

1972 "Identifying the 'Prophet': So, does Jehovah have a prophet to help them, to warn them of dangers and to declare things to come? These questions can be answered in the affirmative. Who is this prophet? . . . This 'prophet' was not one man, but was a body of men and women. It was the small group of footstep followers of Jesus Christ, known at that time as International Bible Students. Today they are known as Jehovah's Christian Witnesses . . . Of course, it is easy to say this group acts as a 'prophet' of God. It is another thing to prove it." *The Watchtower* (4/1/72) (See Deut. 18:21)

The last date the prophet gave for the end was the fall of 1975. After this prophecy failed, the Watchtower Society, as usual, denied it had ever made such a prediction. But by this time, some of the membership was not willing to simply sweep the error under the rug. Some of them wrote to Brooklyn asking why the error was made and why an effort was made to cover it up. One letter from a congregation servant chastised the leaders (think of that!) for not being direct and truthful. Let us not forget at this point that the Watchtower Society claimed, and still claims, to be God's prophet, the only prophet for this time period. There must have been a stirring in Brooklyn. Witnesses there close to home, including the editor and those living and fellowshipping at headquarters, *knew* that the 1975 prediction had been made. They also knew that once again it was erroneous. So, since 1975, several articles have been published attempting to gloss over the error. One article blamed the mistake on the *followers,* indicating that they *misunderstood their leaders.* But the unrest has obviously continued. Finally, in April of 1980, in an article entitled "Choosing the Right Way of Life," the error of 1975 was more freely admitted, that is, in Witness fashion. For the first time as one reads this article carefully, headquarters accepted some, although not all, and in a minor way, responsibility for the error. Could there be those now at Witness headquarters who are challenging the error and challenging false doctrine, which from their vantage point can be so clearly seen?

We might speculate somewhat at this point. After the repeated errors and prediction, the Watchtower Society in its own words, may have learned to stop fixing dates. So, without the fear of impending doom hanging over their heads and without the singular dictatorial leadership of Russell, Rutherford, or Knorr, many Witnesses, including some of the headquarters staff and new members who were not around for the fearsome earlier years, may venture out and accept information and Scripture on their own or from outside sources. Of course, this will be seen as time passes.

13

Testimonies of Ex-Witnesses

Anyone who leaves the society is considered automatically to have joined the evil slave class, and thereby contact with them by Witnesses is prohibited. Witnesses rarely find out what happened to these people. One answer is given for all who leave. They're simply guilty of conduct unbecoming to Christians, and they're written out of Witness life.

But people do leave the movement. David Henke of the Watchman Fellowship reports that from 1969 to 1978, 287,838 people left the organization. When a prominent member leaves the organization, he is simply written off. Hayden C. Covington was high in the organization and his picture was seen in several Witness publications. But several years have passed since he left the Watchtower organization, and there has been no mention of him in any form since.

Henke states that although 124,000 were baptized in 1977, a loss of 1 percent overall was experienced. In the U.S. the loss was 3 percent. Henke also reported that *Watchtower* circulation had decreased by 600,000 to 9,800,000,* and *Awake* magazine circulation decreased 1,225,000. From this information we can form a postulate. If there are two million Witnesses and each one bought five copies of each issue, this would add up to the circulation figure. Of course, all two million would not be active publishers, and some would order a substantial number of maga-

*The October 1980 issue quoted circulating 8,750,000.

76

zines. Another interesting postulate. How many Witnesses' closets are filled with undistributed books and magazines?

A number of ex-Witnesses have written books, made cassette tapes, and given public discourses about their experiences as Jehovah's Witnesses. Some of these who have gained prominence are *Thirty Years a Watchtower Slave,* by William J. Schnell, who served at Brooklyn headquarters; *Released from the Watchtower,* by Valerie Tomsett, an Englishwoman; several testimonies are given in the very fine book by Edmond Gruss entitled *We Left Jehovah's Witnesses, a Non-Prophet Organization.*

There are several active groups that include many ex-Jehovah's Witnesses who minister to Witnesses and other religious groups. One such is the Watchman Fellowship, with several chapters. A family of ex-Witnesses, a husband who had been a Witness for eight years and his wife, a Witness for twenty-two years, came to this fellowship and subsequently joinied a local church in Atlanta. The husband explained their Witness experience. One of his children asked one day why she was not allowed to have a birthday party like the other children. He explained to her that Jehovah's Witnesses didn't favor birthday parties. But he said it stuck in his mind, so he began to look in the Bible. The teaching seemed to have no support in the Scriptures. From this, he began to study more and more, and his doubts began to increase. He explains with emphasis that the only teacher he had was the Bible *at this time* and the Holy Spirit, who was not consulting with Witnesses. His wife would have no part of it for a long time. Finally she also agreed to study and check for herself. So she began to read the Bible and no other publications. In the course of time, she could see more and more clearly the erroneous teachings, and after a real struggle within herself, she also left the movement. It must be added here that one can observe their joy and eagerness. They do appear to be truly released.

Another testimony comes from a twenty-eight-year-old housewife in Alabama. She states that she was reared in a Christian home (not a Jehovah Witness home). She married a young man who was a Witness, and she studied with the Witnesses. She was impressed by their sincerity, their meetings, and their zeal. About two years after her marriage, her mother-in-law, who had been a Witness but who had at this time become disenchanted with the society, was disfellowshipped. The daughter-in-law and her husband then decided to do as the organization instructed and have no association with his mother, nor allow her to see her grandchild. The daughter-in-law already had one doubt about Witness teaching regarding Armageddon that she had harbored for a long time. But now she wondered about this act of disfellowshipping. It did not seem like an act of love. As time passed, more doubts began to develop in her mind. At times, she and her husband would sneak and visit his mother so that the congregation would not find out. They were caught and disciplined by the elders, so they gave up seeing the mother.

As the years passed, she saw more and more displeasing things within the congregation. One point that especially bothered her were the parties held by the Witnesses where some got very drunk. She could not understand this. Then in 1974 the congregation decided that disfellowshipped family members could be spoken to after all, leaving it up to the individual to decide whether or not to speak to a disfellowshipped person, if he or she was not a family member. The parable of the prodigal son was applied. Then she discussed the situation with the overseer at the Kingdom Hall specifically in regard to her mother-in-law. He explained that this parable did not apply to disfellowshipped people. So she began to test the so-called truths of the Watchtower Society. She began to read the Bible and to pray to God to show her the real truth. She had a conversation with her mother-in-law, who gave her a copy of the book, *Why I Left Jehovah's Witnesses* by Ted Dencher. About two months later, she was disfellowshipped. Even though she resigned, they still disfellowshipped her, and they told her she was guilty of idolatry or apostasy, but no reason was given at the Kingdom Hall except conduct unbecoming to Christians.

Included in the appendix is an extensive list of books and

tapes by various people. Although these people have different experiences to relate, all tell of a gradual accumulation of events, discoveries, or doubts that led to their leaving the society. One thing is common to all—they express a newfound joy so overwhelming and so different from any their lives had known prior to that point.

14

The Faithful and Discreet Slave

In the beginning of the movement now called the Watchtower Society of Jehovah's Witnesses, founder Charles T. Russell decided all doctrine and position taken by the society and its members. This matter is thoroughly covered by Buskirk in his book, *The Scholastic Dishonesty of the Watchtower.* He very laboriously and meticulously searched the *Watchtower* literature all the way back to Russell's original writings, so the truth is available regardless of the fact that the society makes a strong effort to distort or destroy these historic facts.

What is the importance of this "slave"? Why do we deal with it in such detail? Witnesses claim the Bible basis for this slave is found in Matthew 24:45-47. In this passage, Jesus gave an example of a good servant or slave whose owner was away. When the owner returned home, he found the good slave doing exactly as he should, so the servant received an appropriate reward. Verses later, Jesus demonstrated an evil servant whose master returned and found him not doing as he should, so he was punished. The Witnesses only deal with the good servant. The verses read: "Who then is a faithful and wise servant, whom his lord hath made ruler over his household, to give them meat in due season? Blessed is that servant, whom his lord when he cometh shall find so doing. Verily I say unto you, that he shall make him ruler over all his goods." The society interprets this to refer specifically to it and no one else. In a very complicated explanation, the Witnesses, since they are the only Christians, make up both the ones who give the food as well as the ones who receive the food. This is hard to follow. They also claim that the slave is a class of people. Those called to the heavenly kingdom are entrusted with great responsibility (*Make Sure of All Things,* page 365). These are the remnant, numbering 144,000 people in all. These are also called the anointed and those having a heavenly hope. As Buskirk points out, Jehovah's Witnesses of today readily accept the society, or, more specifically, those at headquarters who publish the *Watchtower,* as being that servant. But in his day, Russell himself was the slave. This is denied, of course, but the proof is overwhelming.

The central importance of pointing out the giant change in their doctrine lies in the fact that originally the servant was seen to be a single man—Russell. Later they decided it referred to a class (or rather to the organization) and not to a single man. Obviously, after Russell died, they kept dispensing this spiritual food so a new interpretation was needed. Also, the movement was, under Rutherford and especially under Knorr, becoming very organization minded, whereas under Russell, it comprised just Russell and his followers. This can be seen in several quotes from various issues of the *Watchtower* as uncovered by Buskirk: "Jehovah has made understanding the Bible today dependent upon associating with his organization." *Watchtower* (11/1/71), page 668.

"Those who recognize Jehovah's visible theocratic organization, therefore, must recognize and accept this appointment of the faithful and discreet slave and be submissive to it." *Watchtower* (10/1/67), page 590.

"We cannot claim to love God, yet deny his word and channel of communication." *Watchtower* (10/1/78), page 591.

Witnesses are warned against reading literature not published by the society. Buskirk found this astounding quote in the *Watchtower* of August 1, 1950 (p. 231):

> It is good to remember there is only one table of the Lord. Ample supply of excellent food is prepared and served there, and if you know such to be the case, then why go nibbling at the table of those who are opposed to this wise steward

> of the Master's provisions? You might get spiritual poison, for their food has not been theocratically tested. . . . The safest way for God's household is to be content with the food of the Master's providing and as served out by his faithful and wise servant.

Incredible.

Investigation provided another interesting point. In 1881 Russell stated that the servant was not an individual but was the body of Christ, which at that time was not exclusively Jehovah's Witnesses. But we see from the record that he changed his mind and decided that he actually was the slave. Rutherford later agreed until he realized the need to change his view in order to hold the group together. Russell's wife may have been first to state that her husband was the servant. The *Watchtower* of December 1, 1916, stated that thousands of readers believed that Russell filled the office of that servant, and "although his modesty and humility prevented his claiming his title openly, he admitted that he was in private conversation." *Watchtower* publications insist he never said he was the servant. It is amazing that this so-called Christian organization would print such lies and so many falsehoods. Even though their membership does not have access to older books published, headquarters does. It is difficult to understand why *someone* there does not expose the real truth.

Of all the doctrine of the Watchtower Society, this one (the "slave") needs most study of all. It is this force, this fear, which keeps all the members in line, keeps them listening, and keeps them obedient. Articles in the *Watchtower* warn followers against reading literature the society doesn't publish. (We will read it for you, and if you need to know any of it, we will condense it for you and print it.) Likewise, listening to radio preachers also is criticized.

Christendom is a term they have coined which literally includes everybody else but the Witnesses. All churches of Christendom are described as hypocritical, pretensive, spewing false doctrine, and connected in some way with the politics and economic systems of the world. There is not one group outside the Witnesses who is in any way recommended. All are wrong and all are doomed. Now, particularly understand this point; no Witnesses ever investigate these facts. They absolutely fear the society to such a strong degree, even if they won't admit that it's true. They will not, under any circumstances, attend the worship service of any other church. If a Witness attends the funeral of a friend or relative who is not a Jehovah's Witness, and the service is conducted by someone from Christendom, the Witness will sit quietly but with his mind blocking the message, and he will not join in any prayer. In fact, he will not join in any prayer not led by a Jehovah's Witness because of the fear that the prayer is not to the real God. Think of that! In their complete blindness under society teaching, Witnesses think that no one else in all the world has access to the great, mighty, loving God (who so loved the world).

More needs to be said about the slave. It is necessary to point out clearly the change from *Russell* the slave to the *organization* the slave. This shows that the society has positively interpreted the passage in Matthew two ways, and, strangely enough, the change in interpretation happened to fit a need at a critical time in their history. But let us here clear up the matter and present proof positive that they did positively change the interpretation. The following quotations are taken directly from *Watchtower* literature.

> The Lord gave the harvest message to the Laodician church, the faithful ones of whom composed the "feet members" of Christ; and he gave it through his especially chosen servant, according to His promise (Matt, 24:45-47). All the "feet members" who are now engaged in proclaiming this precious message received their enlightenment by partaking of the "food" which the Lord sent through his chosen servant. The *Watchtower* unhesitatingly proclaims Brother Russell as that faithful and wise servant. (*The Watchtower and Herald of Christ's Presence*, 3/1/81)

Can there be any doubt from this quote that the *Watchtower* publishers at least stated and believed, as a matter of fact, unhesitatingly said, that Brother Russell was that faithful and wise servant? You can't misinterpret or distort such a direct quote.

> Shall we, then, continue to recognize in our class studies the Berean Bible lessons prepared by Brother Russell? Shall we continue to speak in our class studies of Brother Russell as the Lord's servant who brought "meat in due season to the household of faith"? Yes, indeed. Why not? If the Lord was pleased to use him for many years to give the "meat in due season," then the Berean Bible lessons are essential for the development of those who shall be made partakers of the kingdom. Should we now disregard the food contained in the *Studies in the Scriptures* and other publications of the Watchtower Bible and Tract Society, it would mean that we were repudiating or disregarding that which the Lord has graciously provided for our benefit. We must make distinction between Brother Russell as a creature and his official capacity as "that servant" of the Master to give out the "meat in due season." To disregard the message would mean to disregard the Lord . . . The Lord's faithful and wise servant finished his work and left us with his message.

> *The Watchtower.* This publication is a medium through which the kingdom message is brought regularly to the members of the "household." "That servant" used this medium to give out the "meat in due season." By his last will and testament he provided for the continuance of the *Watchtower* by a duly constituted editorial committee.

This quote is taken directly from the *Watchtower* of December 15, 1916. At this point, Russell had been dead two months, and the future was indeed much in doubt. But there is no doubt about the official recognition by the Watchtower Society that Russell in fact was viewed as that "servant."

So it is absolutely clear that the society officers, *Watchtower* editors, and Judge Rutherford himself had at one point for several years accepted and declared Russell to be the one who gave the food (or instruction, interpretation, and explanation) of Scripture and prophecy. The point was repeated over and over that the servant (singular) simply could not be interpreted to mean more than one person, indicating it could not be the whole body of Christ.

Now, please note carefully, if Russell had in fact fulfilled the prophecy as claimed and declared, how could the followers of today claim actually the opposite? They say now that the "servant" meant or means, in fact, a certain *group*. The Witnesses in Russell's day and shortly after said the servant could not by any means be interpreted to mean anything other than one man: "However much we might endeavor to apply this figure to the Lord's people collectively, the fact would still remain that the various items stated would not fit into a company of individuals" (*Watchtower,* April 15, 1904, p. 125).

So, a review of *Watchtower* literature at the time of, and after, Russell's death shows us how and why the slave was changed. It is somewhat ironic that the organization Russell founded eventually almost disassociated from his name. *Watchtower* literature now gives Russell brief attention and rarely publishes the details of his leadership. However, Russell's influence cannot be denied. One of the names by which Witnesses were known for a time was "Russellites," a name not well accepted by the organization and a cause of anger to them today.

Russell provided in his will for the continuance of the publication of the *Watchtower*. He spelled out in detail his instructions to ensure its continuation. After he died, an executive committee of three men, including J. F. Rutherford, was appointed to manage the affairs of the society until the annual election in January of 1917. This was late in 1916. Although nothing has been uncovered to indicate that Russell preferred Rutherford as his successor (his major concern seems to have been that the publishing of his materials be continued), after a considerable battle, Rutherford took charge. A. H. MacMillan, who was an officer in the organization at that time, seems to indicate in his book that Russell may have preferred *him* for the job.

At this point we begin to see a great change taking place in the organization. The personality of Rutherford replaced that of Russell, and Witnesses since Rutherford's day saw themselves as governed by what is called the theocracy, meaning God's rule as opposed to, for example, a democracy where people rule. Quotations from the *Watchtower* are ample proof of the evolved change in the theocracy. Buskirk's research provides the following:

> The church on this side of the veil is made up of various ecclesias or classes scattered throughout the earth. Each ecclesia or class is a body in itself representing the Lord. And it has control over the affairs of that particular body. In accordance with the Scriptures, that ecclesia elects its elders, its deacons and other servants of the church, each one having his respective office to perform. We believe that all will agree that such is a divine arrangement. . . . The literature when printed is sent to the classes for distribution. No one is compelled to engage in the distribution of the literature and if any individual feels that he cannot consciously distribute he ought not do so. (*Watchtower*, May 1, 1921, p. 135)

Now, notice this date. Russell had been gone for about three years. The theocracy thus described is a far cry from the present organization as Witnesses know it today. All talks must follow outlines sent from headquarters. Questions, as well as answers, are supplied for all study materials. Witnesses are told exactly whom to worship, how to worship, what to read, and they are forbidden any personal or private interpretation of anything. If one crosses the society, he either apologizes or is disfellowshipped. Witnesses are taught to put aside all doubts and uncertainties and to simply trust the organization in all matters.

In their most recent books and literature, Witnesses use the terminology "put faith in a victorious organization," the incoming "world government." It doesn't say Jehovah here, does it? All allegiance is directed toward the *organization* (the slave, remember?). We know Witnesses are told how and what to think in all matters of religion. Even the particular songs they sing are ordered from Brooklyn. (Witnesses say this isn't so.)

After Russell died, many Russellites left who had clung to his teachings and who truly saw him as the "faithful servant" of God. Bitter infighting for power ensued. Some were disillusioned and fell away; others made strong efforts to see that the movement Russell started continued. The organization was shaken. Marley Cole, in his book *Jehovah's Witnesses,* states:

But after forty years of listening to his sermons and studying under his tutelage Bible students found themselves too shocked, too stunned by the loss of him to know in what direction to go. At any rate many of them felt that way. They seemed to think that further revelation had died out with the pastor. An editorial writer through the *Watchtower* had to reassure the faithful in 1917 that the sermons still being run in the magazine were the pastor's sermons. (p. 82)

Rutherford realized he had to turn their attention away from Russell. "Creature worship," he told the organization, must be avoided. He said that since 1914 brought in the kingdom, then they must get busy and advertise. In other words, let's get our minds on something else. But, as Cole continues, "This didn't appeal too well to a big segment of listeners. For forty years they had looked forward to 1914. Many of them felt that by October of that year the Lord would come down and sweep them off to heaven in glory. He failed to come that way."

Now why did this large group of Russell's followers think Jesus would come for them in 1914? Most certainly all of them could not have misunderstood. One of Russell's top aides, A. H. MacMillan, admitted in his book, *Faith on the March,* that he himself, an officer in the society, expected to be carried off into heaven in 1914. So the modern organization cannot hide the fact that it learned this from Russell. To simply state that "all that was expected to happen didn't happen" is dishonest and deceptive.

Under Rutherford's leadership, the seventh volume of *Studies in the Scriptures* left incomplete at Russell's death was completed and published. This was exactly what Rutherford needed. As Cole said, "It was a triumph for the organization" (p. 85). The book was released in 1917 (Russell died in October of 1916). A commentary on Revelation and Ezekiel, the book raised an international furor in the United States and Canada. Catholics, Protestants, politics, economics were all linked together and called "Babylon." In other words, the book developed a "them vs. us" position as though there were only two groups of people in the world—the Bible students still not yet called Jehovah's Witnesses on the one side, and everyone else on the other.

Rutherford joined the Russell movement in 1906 and the next year became their lawyer. As previously mentioned a search of Russell's writings does not reveal his desire that Rutherford succeed him, but Rutherford got the job. According to a report in a *Watchtower* of that time, Rutherford received a very large majority of votes by the membership. However, it appears he had a real battle at headquarters. He began to reorganize. A full-scale rebellion broke out in Brooklyn. Four of the seven directors challenged Rutherford less than six months after he came into office. MacMillan, who may have been Russell's choice for a successor, was appointed by Rutherford to be the president's aide. The four directors wanted the board to have more authority, but Rutherford, as did Russell, was proceeding as he desired without consultation or authority from the board. A political power struggle developed and Rutherford won. MacMillan reports that at one point a policeman was called in to maintain peace. By use of a technicality, which Russell had always ignored, Rutherford replaced all four complainers (as he called them) with his supporters. A large number eventually left the organization. Some voluntarily and some not. From this action a number of splinter groups evolved.

Rutherford was gaining power. The seventh volume of *Studies in the Scriptures* depicted the fall of Babylon, such to take place very soon. This scorching work, released during the time the nations were at war, caused a groundswell of indignation in the governments of Canada and the United States. *Watchtower* publications were banned in Canada in 1918. William Schnell, an ex-Witness now but a Witness then, claims that Rutherford conducted a seemingly antiwar policy. Later in the same year, the United States government arrested Rutherford and others on charges of refusing to serve in the military. They were imprisoned in Atlanta, Georgia. Organization work stopped. The war ended in November, 1918, and Rutherford was freed. His conviction was overturned the next year. Rutherford capitalized on this and said that Scripture was fulfilled by this action.

One of Rutherford's most revealing works was a book called

Preparation. Here he dealt with the difficulties of the society, his problem in assuming command from within the ranks, and the problems brought on from publishing the seventh volume of *Studies in the Scriptures.* Rutherford always seemed to find some Scriptures here and there in support. Beginning on page 286 of *Preparation,* he states that Christendom, which Rutherford said was made up of Great Britain and the United States, attacked the organization. The attackers were called Satan's agents and they "fled the houses" and seized organization property. The organization is described by Rutherford as the chaste virgin who was humiliated by these agents of Satan. Some, said Rutherford, held fast, that is, the faithful ones. Recall now that this was happening during the period of unrest at headquarters. But others become unfaithful and went back into the world and became members of the evil servant class. Rutherford next presents an absolutely fascinating, incredible interpretation of Zechariah 14. Read Zechariah. Investigate all the commentaries you can find or anything helpful and see if there's any way you could believe this distortion.

God's organization on earth, says Rutherford, is the city spoken of in Zechariah 14. The story begins after Satan's agents, Canada and the United States, release the society. Rutherford describes those who oppose him: "These being no longer virgins become ravaged by Satan's organization, are therefore unclean, and they are not permitted to enter the house of the Lord" (p. 288). Since a portion of the verse says "half of the city shall go forth into captivity," Rutherford developed his theory. The whole quote says, "For I will gather all the nations against Jerusalem to battle; and the city shall be taken, and the houses rifled, and the women ravished; and half of the city shall go forth into captivity, and the residue of the people shall not be cut off from the city." Rutherford explained this to mean that the organization was separated into two divisions. Let us quote Rutherford: "Of that entire company or organization symbolized by the city, one part goes into the evil servant class while the other part the Lord uses to make up the faithful and wise servant class (Matt. 24:45-51)." The clear inference here to be drawn from this language of Zechariah's prophecy is that the one part that went into captivity is cut off completely from God's organization. Rutherford explains further that those cut off can *never* come back in, but become the evil servant class. Think of it. Those who sincerely opposed Rutherford were cut off forever from the organization or, to put it another way, from God. Is this vicious and vengeful? Surely it warned the fence sitters. If this were not so serious it would be humorous. But thousands believed this man, so it isn't funny at all; it is very sad.

Rutherford finished this saga of prophecy by explaining that this affected only those in the organization in 1918 when Jesus appeared at the temple. On page 290, this remaining half of the city joined with those of the Ruth-Esther class, and all these became the remnant. This is a very important word. This group, cleansed and made part of the temple organization, was a special class headed by Jesus that constitutes the people of God.

On page 291, we find that Jehovah *stopped the World War in 1918 so that the remnant could prepare for the battle of Armageddon just around the corner.* These ones under Christ, says Rutherford, are anointed and sent forth to preach before the final battle is fought. They are the real earthly enemies of Satan (p. 292). Let us review: It started with the city. It split in half. This was caused by Satan's agents, Canada and the United States. The bad half joined with Satan and is lost forever from God. The good half stuck with Rutherford and stayed in the organization, doing as they were told and yielding to the meat now coming from Rutherford instead of Russell, and all this fulfilled the prophecy of Zechariah. The ones who disagreed with Rutherford became the *evil slave class* and the followers of Rutherford became the *faithful and discreet slave class.* Present-day Witnesses will notice right away that the "other sheep" apparently had not been discovered, but a class called Jonadabs, who represented or foreshadowed that class of people now on earth who are of goodwill and "out of harmony" with Satan's organization. These take their stand on the side of righteousness, and they are the ones whom, if obedient and faithful, the Lord will preserve during the time of Armageddon, take them through their trouble, and give them everlasting life on earth (*Riches,* 1936). In other words, these were people of goodwill, not Jehovah's Witnesses, not the remnant, but not condemned.

Rutherford moved with deliberate speed and established the organization as the slave until eventually it was forgotten by the membership that Russell was ever represented as the slave, and in ensuing years, repeated articles reminded the Witnesses of the need to heed without question the information, instructions, and orders given by the slave, which they must in honesty admit is looked upon by the average Witness as the rest of the 144,000 left on earth, now about 10,000 people. But the meat they give is dispersed by a far smaller number located at the Brooklyn headquarters. The congregation is encouraged to, but in fact it absolutely must, give total allegiance to the slave. They must put faith in "a victorious organization" (*Watchtower,* 3/1/79, p. 12). Not faith in God, mind you. The same *Watchtower* issue contains an article entitled "To Whom Shall We Go but Jesus Christ?" Here's how the article tells one to go to Jesus Christ:

> When telling about his presence and the end of the system of things, Jesus assures his followers that he would appoint the faithful and discreet slave that would care for his interests and feed his followers down through the Christian epoch with food at the proper time. Proving faithful, this slave class would be appointed by Jesus at his Second Coming over all his belongings. Yes, also by means of his faithful and discreet slave Jesus has been with his followers. Matt. 24:45-47 (p. 20)

We have included this Scripture along with the quote. Make no mistake. The original slave was Russell. The second slave was Rutherford. The third slave is the small group in Brooklyn who leads this organization.

15

Watching the Watchtower Organization Change

The organization was not always an organization. It became an organization through the mind and act of J. F. Rutherford. In the beginning it was Russell and his followers. Here is a chronological series of events. Russell had a childhood fear of hell. The teenage Russell left the church and became an agnostic. He came upon the Second Adventists and liked their teaching, and soon he began to write about the Bible. Then there were joint writings by Russell and Barber. Russell disagreed about the return of Jesus Christ and went out on his own to start a class of six members.

Russell began to write down his views about the Bible. He felt sure Jesus would return in 1874. In other words, as they teach today, the day was upon them. It was urgent; the Jews were returning to Palestine, which was a sure sign of the end. All signs definitely indicated that Armageddon would occur in 1914. Since the world did not end in 1914, Russell discovered that 1914 was only the beginning of the end, but still the end was very close. All the *Watchtower* publications declared it. *Studies in the Scriptures* proved it. At this point, there was no organization as such; there was just Russell and his followers. No one thought at this time that God had an organization, nor did they even consider it. The followers did think Russell had direct revelation from God.

When Russell died, his movement almost died. He had taken steps to assure the continued publishing of his sermons, but he had no plans to start an organization such as eventually developed. In fact, Russell's books held that there were Christians, although misguided, in the various denominations. Rutherford battled his way to leadership of the *Watchtower* publishing company. Russell, however, had not picked Rutherford to succeed him. The organization almost folded. Many left and many took exception to Rutherford.

Rutherford at first continued as started by Russell, but soon he changed the identity of the slave from Russell the man to a group, the group, that is, that *he* now headed. This marked the beginning of the organization. Individual rights of the congregations or ecclesias were steadily removed. Rutherford warned that they must shape up or ship out, and a number of them shipped out. World War I came. Rutherford directed the attention of his people to the war. Soon he was in jail and a hero. He told them that Christ came to the temple in 1918, which was foretold in the cleansing of the organization. Now there really was an organization, but it was Rutherford, just as before it was Russell. Rutherford now wrote all the doctrine "correcting" Russell when required. Any love left was replaced by duty, fear, and obligation.

Rutherford began to draw the line between him and his followers and everybody else, which was a change from even his own early writings. He blasted religion, declaring his was not by any means a religion. As a matter of fact, he lumped the churches, commerce, and politics into one group, which takes some doing! And he announced that they all were opposed to the Witnesses. Actually, it was the other way around. Churches, finance, and politics gave and still give little attention to the Witnesses other than to honor their right to be a religion for tax-exemption purposes. Who attacked whom? Rutherford sent followers into the communities to oppose the draft, war, and patriotism. Witnesses were taught not to waste time going to school and being educated. Yet they themselves need lawyers, doctors, and typists.

Toward the end of Rutherford's rule, the organization was really becoming just that—an organization. The emphasis on the individual began to change radically. No society books after Rutherford bear the name of the author. Early on, Knorr's picture was seen in a *Watchtower* publication. When he died, only a brief mention was made. His successor was barely mentioned at all. So now there really is an organization. They call it the theocracy and also now call themselves a religion—*the* religion, in fact. Here's how they see themselves now. The organization has two meanings. It means a small group in Brooklyn who write the books. It also is used to mean every Jehovah's Witness. They see themselves both as the giver of meat in due season as well as the receiver of the meat. There's only one other organization. It is called Christendom and at times called Babylon. Everybody else belongs to this group of the Devil, and this group is diabolically opposed to the theocracy. They will one day very soon, they keep claiming over, and over, clash at the battle they now call Harmageddon (they used to say Armageddon). They will not have to fight because Jesus, as chief soldier of Jehovah, will do the battle. This battle has been at the doors repeatedly at different times throughout history but always urgently just ahead. The organization is the ark of safety. There is no other ark. No one may reach the Father unless he goes by way of the theocracy. Ask any one of them if this is so. They have the only Truth, the only contact.

What's that you say? You don't see this theocracy in the Bible? Let's look again. You are right. It isn't in the Bible. It is a serious, highly responsible act to undertake to declare the route of access to God. We all do agree that there is only one way. Is this in the Bible? It is in the Bible. Is it hard to find out or hard to interpret? No, it is very clear and very distinctive. It is in John 14. Jesus is describing the place he will prepare and Thomas said that they didn't know the way to get there. Jesus said, "I am the way, the truth and the life. No one comes to the Father, but by me." Jesus did not mention the Baptists, Methodists, or a theocracy. What a severe truth emerges here. No one, no theocracy can supersede or in any way change the fact that Jesus is the way. Witnesses, pray about this. God will not fail you. Don't pray to the theocracy. Don't you see? There is nothing there. Pray to God and claim Jesus' redemption personally for yourself. Then prepare for your new life in Christ. You will never be the same. But for the first time you will know at last that you are in the presence of God himself. You *can go around* the organization. God is waiting, try it. You don't need an audience. You don't need an intercessor. You don't need headquarters. Just begin direct confession. "Dear God, I confess my sins. I confess my failure to accept the atonement of Jesus Christ for me. Teach me your truth about Jesus Christ. Free me from all snares and interferences." Start this prayer believing. The rest will come from you. Then get ready for a wave of peace and joy such as you have never ever known. Then you'll come to the real organization, the brotherhood of God. Amen.

Epilogue

SPECULATIONS

Review of the history of the Watchtower Society shows that this movement began in the mind and the efforts of Charles Taze Russell about 100 years ago. It was a rebellion against the Christian doctrine of Russell's day (which doctrine has not ever changed although Russell's doctrine has changed many times). It is certain that the Watchtower Society has learned much through its error. For instance, in earlier days specific interpretations of prophecy such as dates of events were published and heavily promoted. Now, as the society's literature says, it is learning to stop fixing dates. According to its doctrine of the fifties, the Watchtower Society decided it should give "less attention" to Jesus. Earlier *Watchtower* literature used terms such as "cross of Christ" and "blood of Christ." Salvation by His blood was emphasized. But since the fifties the "cross" has been replaced by "torture-stake."

The pamphlet "Our Kingdom Service," April, 1979, said that Jesus has "aided us to receive the greatest gift anyone can obtain, everlasting life." Jesus' role over the years was clearly reduced, but now it seems to be becoming more prominent again in the literature. There are references toward looking for His Second Coming (or presence), and there seems to be an effort to cloud the meaning presently applied so that one may "believe like they used to" or "believe like they are going to." The Holy Spirit, explained by Witness doctrine as God's active force, is now seen in the literature to indwell and teach believers.

It may be that some of the society's present leaders are

looking more into Scripture and are reaching new views. Not to be outdone by others, *Watchtower* literature now allows that at least some can be "born again." And the literature of 1980 emphasizes such subjects as how to have a happy home, child rearing, and drug abuse. There is less doctrine and much milder attack on others. In fact, there is little similarity between the literature of 1980 and the scalding literature of earlier years.

So there is some evidence that the Watchtower Society may be moving closer toward the *real* truth. The society is no longer under dictatorial leadership, and speculation could be made that the broader-based, younger, more diverse leadership simply is unwilling to accept and continue the materials and positions they know to be erroneous and not of their own understanding scriptural.

There is strong and growing evidence that there is much discord at Bethel and that more than a few members of the Bethel family are challenging the errors and organizational procedures. The press has become interested and numerous articles are appearing in newspapers and magazines. A recent article in *Newsweek* magazine reported about Raymond Franz, a life-long member of the society, author of major books such as *Aid to Bible Understanding,* a member of the governing body said to be in line to replace the present leader, Frederick Franz, Raymond's uncle. Raymond Franz, during Bible research for some of the books he authored, discovered that Scripture did not agree with certain doctrine of the society. He tried to reason with the hierarchy about these problems with no success. In fact, he was removed from his position at Bethel and later was disfellowshipped from the organization because he was "seen eating" in a restaurant with another disfellowshipped witness, Peter Gregerson, who also had been a ranking officer in the society. Mr. Gregerson has appeared on radio, and the things he tells are hardly congruent with a "loving" organization. Newspapers report considerable rebellion in Canada, also involving a prominent ex-Witness (James Penton), and a number of members have left the congregation in Canada. Two men who have recently left Bethel tell of the trouble there. Independent Bible studies were being held by various small Bethel groups and attempts have been made to squash these studies. These two men provide considerable insight into previously unknown facts about life at Bethel and about certain of their leaders. Mr. Gregerson says that he was told that almost none of the members of the governing body believe all the doctrine they expound.

Could this be the dawning of a new Watchtower Society? The dynamism of this organization could be turned into a mighty force for real truth, but first it must come to accurate knowledge of the deity of, and proper relationship with, their and our Lord Jesus Christ.

Appendixes

SPIRITUAL ISRAEL

Who is the *Watchtower* talking about?

"Similarly nominal spiritual Israel has neglected the counsel of this Golden Text, and instead of having the Lord first, has been disposed to forget the Lord and to affiliate with the world, to seek worldly favor and cooperation."

December 1, 1904

MILLIONS NOW LIVING WILL NEVER DIE

This is the title of a book by J. F. Rutherford written in 1920. This book contains his prophecy that Abraham, Isaac, Jacob, and others would be resurrected and would return to live and rule on this earth in 1925. This book also prophesied the establishment of New Israel in Palestine at the same time.

Millions Now Living Will Never Die is an opportunity for newer Witnesses to learn something of the mind-set of their second leader, J. F. Rutherford.

A copy of this book may be ordered from C.A.R.I.S., P. O. Box 1783, Santa Ana, California 92702. The price per copy is $4.00.

RUSSELL SAID

". . . full establishment of the Kingdom of God in the earth at A.D. 1914" (*Thy Kingdom Come,* 1907 edition).

". . . full establishment of the Kingdom of God in the earth after A.D. 1914" (*Thy Kingdom Come*, 1925 edition).

". . . full establishment of the Kingdom of God will be accomplished near the end of A.D. 1915" (*The Time Is at Hand*, 1920 edition).

"John 14:3 certainly referred to a second personal coming" (*Studies in the Scriptures*, vol. I).

RUTHERFORD SAID

That God's favor returned to the Jew for restoration of the nation of Israel in 1918.[1]

That a number of good ministers of the gospel met in London.[1] (These "good ministers" were not in any way Jehovah's Witnesses.)

The sun represents the gospel of Jesus Christ and him crucified.[1]

Passing the collection plate is an honorable way for a church to raise money.[1]

John Bunyan was a humble follower of Jesus. Rutherford said that Bunyan's book, *Pilgrim's Progress*, has been a great comfort and help to Christians.[1] (Do you know what this book was about?)

Jesus is *the* (Rutherford used "the," not "a") mighty God.[1]

The year 1925 would see the return to earthly life of Abraham, Isaac, and Jacob.[1]

The babe Jesus is thus identified as the One whom God has selected as his king and head of his kingdom. Witnesses today are taught that Jesus was baptized before anyone was sure He was Messiah.[2] It is now certain that the greatest storm or time

[1]*Millions Now Living Will Never Die*
[2]*What You Need*

of trouble ever known is rapidly coming upon the world.[2] (This
was said in 1932.)

ARMAGEDDON IS COMING, IS COMING
IS COMING, IS COMING

1.*   *1877*   "The end of this world . . . is nearer than most
men suppose."

2.   *1886*   "Marshalling of the hosts for the battle of the
great day of God Almighty is in progress."

3.   *1889*   "The 'battle of the great day of God Almighty,' . . .
which will end in 1914 . . . is already commenced."

4.   *1894*   "The skirmishing is already beginning all along the
line." "The end of 1914 is not the date for the
beginning, but for the end of the time of trouble."

5.   *1904*   "The stress of the great time of trouble will be on
us soon, somewhere between 1910 and 1912—cul-
minating . . . October 1914."

6.   *1914*   "The great crisis, the great clash . . . is very near."
"Armageddon may begin next spring."

7.   *1915*   "The Battle of Armageddon, to which this war is
leading . . ."

8.   *1915*   "The present great war in Europe is the beginning
of the Armageddon of the Scriptures."

9.   *1917*   "We anticipate that the 'earthquake' will occur
early in 1918, and that the 'fire' will come in the
fall of 1920."

10.   *1920*   "The old order of things, the old world, is ending."
"Deliverance is at the door."

11.   *1929*   "God's purpose now to shortly clash to pieces the
Devil's organization."

*Numbers 1 through 28 from Edmond Gruss, *Jehovah's Witnesses and
Prophetic Speculation.*

"Satan that shortly he must fight the Lord."

12.	*1930*	"The great climax is at hand."
13.	*1931*	"His day of vengeance is here, and Armageddon is at hand."

"God's judgment must shortly be executed."

14.	*1932*	"The end a short time away."
15.	*1939*	"The disaster of Armageddon is just ahead."
16.	*1940*	"The day for final settlement is near at hand."

"The Witness work for the theocracy appears to be about done."

17.	*1941*	"Armageddon is surely near . . . within a few years."
18.	*1942*	"The New World is at the doors. . . . The time is short."
19.	*1943*	"The beginning of the final war is dangerously near."
20.	*1944*	"The end of the world arrangement is now near."
21.	*1946*	"Armageddon should come sometime before 1972."
22.	*1950*	"Jehovah's time has come to settle definitely the issue."
23.	*1953*	"1954 could well be 'The Year.' "
24.	*1955*	"The war of Armageddon is nearing its breaking out point."
25.	*1966*	"A climax of man's history is at the door."
26.	*1968*	"Why are you looking forward to 1975?"
27.	*1969*	"There is only a short time left."
28.	*1975*	F. W. Franz: "After September 5, things could happen, according to the way that affairs are going in the world. . . . So it could come quickly, within a short time after the terminal day of the lunar year 1975. And we should not jump to wrong decisions on that account and say, well, the time after September 5, 1975, is indefinitely long and so it will allow for me to [get] married and [raise] a family. . . . No! the time does not allow for that, dear friends. . . . Evidently there is not much time left."

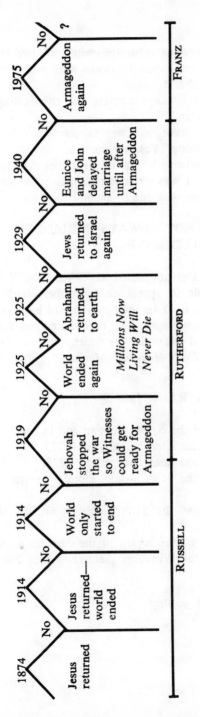

Riding the Waves of Witness Error

1874	No	1914	No	1914	No	1919	No	1925	No	1925	No	1929	No	1940	No	1975	No
Jesus returned		Jesus returned— world ended		World only started to end		Jehovah stopped the war so Witnesses could get ready for Armageddon		World ended again		Abraham returned to earth		Jews returned to Israel again		Eunice and John delayed marriage until after Armageddon		Armageddon again	?

Millions Now Living Will Never Die

RUSSELL   RUTHERFORD   FRANZ

Both Russell and Rutherford felt sure the climactic events of history would occur during his own lifetime, and they both interpreted Scripture accordingly. Almost all the date-setting was done by these two men, as the chart indicates. Since Knorr's time date-fixing has been more vague, the only specific date being 1975.

29.   *1977*   "It is obvious from the events of our times that the present wicked system will soon receive its death blow."*

30.   *1978*   "We are fast approaching the culminating feature of the 'sign.' "†

31.   *1980*   "Do we have any way of knowing the time of Armageddon? Yes, we do."

"The evidence is just as clear that Armageddon is near as it was clear earlier this year that Mount St. Helens was due to erupt."**

WITNESSES WERE NOT ALWAYS FORBIDDEN TO CELEBRATE BIRTHDAYS

For a time a booklet advertised as "What You Have Long Wanted" was available for purchase from the Watchtower. It was suggested that this book be used as a record book of friends, their birthdays, and autographs. The book contained a table for ascertaining the day of the week on which one was born. The title of the book was *Daily Heavenly Manna*.

ERRORS AND CONTRADICTIONS

1.   Russell calculated the 6,000 years to end in 1872.
2.   The calculation was later changed to 1972.
3.   The calculation was later changed to 1975.
4.   Russell thought the Jews would literally return to Israel by 1914.
5.   Rutherford thought the Jews would return to Israel by 1925.
6.   Rutherford changed the return of the Jews to a "spiritual" return, meaning the Witnesses themselves, not literal Jews.

*Watchtower, 4/1/77, p. 199.
†Watchtower, 1/15/78, p. 10.
**Watchtower, 12/1/80.

7. Russell was the original slave.
8. Rutherford said Russell indeed was the slave, then changed the slave to mean the organization.
9. Russell predicted (prophesied) the "end" for 1914. Rutherford was so sure the end would come in 1925 that he had a house built for Abraham and David to live in.
10. Under Knorr, the Watchtower Society decided to stop fixing dates. However, the membership was led to believe that 1975 was the end.
11. Witnesses hope they have pleased Jehovah, but none are sure of salvation. Yet 1 John 5 says one *can* know for sure.
12. Russell determined the end time to be 1874 by measuring the Great Pyramid of Egypt. After it did not happen, Russell remeasured and this time the date was 1914.
13. Russell said in *Studies in the Scriptures* that the gospel had already been preached in all the lands, so the end could come in 1914 as he prophesied.
14. Rutherford said in 1940 that the time was too short to marry.
15. Franz said in 1975 that there was no time left for marriage and college.
16. The *Watchtower* (10/1/78, p. 10), said it is proper to go ahead and marry.

CHRISTMAS

Watchtower, Dec. 15, 1903: "Upon this day so generally celebrated, we may properly join with all whose hearts are in the attitude of love and appreciation toward God and the Saviour."

Watchtower, Nov. 15, 1907, suggested that *Studies in the Scriptures* be given as Christmas gifts.

President Rutherford thanked his followers for Christmas gifts to him in the *Watchtower,* Jan. 15, 1919.

Watchtower, Dec. 15, 1926: "The event [Christmas] is so important, that it is always appropriate to call it to the minds of the people, regardless of the date."

Watchtower, Dec. 1, 1904: "We may as well join with the civilized world in celebrating the grand event on the day which the majority celebrate—Christmas day. The lesson for the occasion is a most happy choice, fitting well to the series of lessons it follows." This lesson was titled "Prince of Peace" and was prepared for December 25.

Yearbook, 1975: Russell and the Bethel family had a Christmas tree, celebrated Christmas, and, including Russell, exchanged gifts.

THE FLAG

DID YOU KNOW THIS WAS IN THE WATCHTOWER?

Watchtower, May 15, 1917: "To those who love liberty and peace, the flag represents liberty and peace . . . respect to the government under which it is the privilege of Christians to live . . . everyone in America should take pleasure in displaying the American flag."

"Since the Bethel home was established, in one end of the drawing room there has been kept a small bust of Abraham Lincoln with two American flags displayed about the bust . . . and in this we see nothing inconsistent with a Christian's duty."

Jehovah's Witnesses feel that they are in "the truth" if they are in "the organization"

But

Jesus Christ said that *He* is the truth

So

To be in the truth, we must be in Christ. He didn't mention any organizations.

That's different.

IT IS A FACT THAT YOU CAN BE
SAVED AND KNOW IT

"He that believeth on the Son of God hath the witness in himself: he that believeth not God hath made him a liar; because he believeth not the record that God gave of His Son. And this is the record, that God hath given to us eternal life, and this life is in His Son. *He that hath the Son hath life; and he that hath not the Son of God hath not life. These things have I written unto you that believe on the name of the Son of God;* THAT YE MAY KNOW THAT YE HAVE ETERNAL LIFE, *and that ye may believe on the name of the Son of God.*" 1 John 5:10-13

IT IS A FACT THAT YOU CAN BE SAVED
BY FAITH IN JESUS CHRIST

"Sirs, what must I do to be saved? *And they said, Believe on the Lord Jesus Christ, and thou shalt be saved, and thy house.*" Acts 16:30-31

THE WORKS OF GOD

"What shall we do, that we might work the works of God? Jesus answered and said unto them, This is the work of God, that ye believe on him whom he hath sent." John 6:28-29

THE TRUTH

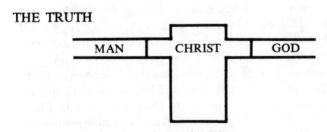

I am the Way.
No one come to the Father except by me.

The real truth is that only Jesus Christ can bridge the chasm of separation between man and Jehovah. *No other*—not the *Watchtower,* the Southern Baptist, the Presbyterian—no other can bridge this gap. Salvation comes only by the cross of Jesus Christ.

"Neither is there salvation in any other: for there is none other name under heaven given among men, whereby *we must be saved.*" Acts 4:12

"As ye have therefore received Christ Jesus the Lord, so walk ye in him. . . . Beware lest any man spoil you through philosophy and vain deceit, after the tradition of men, after the rudiments of the world, *and not after Christ.* For in him dwelleth all the full-ness of the Godhead bodily. And *ye are complete in him,* which is the head of all principality and power." Colossians 2:6, 8-10

THE THIRTY-DAY TEST

Question: Is it true that Jehovah's Witnesses consider the Bible to be the dependable Word of God? Is all Witness doctrine based absolutely on this Word? Does the Watchtower Society encourage the reading of the Bible?

A challenge: Take the thirty-day test. This means that for thirty consecutive days you will read *only* the Bible and no other religious literature from any source. During this time, pray to Jehovah for guidance, direction, and teaching. Open yourself to Jehovah directly and earnestly. Talk to God about your desire to be in the real truth and how you have felt this truth to be inside the society. Express a genuine, sincere willingness to accept whatever God reveals directly to you. Then, *listen to God speak to you.* You know that it is proper to *claim* the *blood* of Christ! Do it! If you do this in earnest seeking, something wonderful awaits you! Try it!

I am not skilled to understand
what God has willed, what God has planned.
I only know at His right hand
is One who is my Saviour.

I take Him at His word indeed.
Christ died for sinners, this I read.
And in my heart I find a need
for Him to be my Saviour.

That He should leave His throne on high
and come for sinners and to die—
YOU COUNT THAT STRANGE? well, once, did I
before I knew my Saviour.

—Dora Greenwell, 1873

LOVING HELP FOR JEHOVAH'S WITNESSES

The ministries listed below will be pleased and honored to write, send materials, or help to contact a friend in any community. Confidentiality will be protected. There are also other ministries in the U.S. and Canada.

The Watchman Fellowship
P.O. Box 7681
Columbus, Ga. 31908

MacGregor Ministries
P.O.Box 1215
Delta, B.C. V4M3T3

Rev. Maurice Coveney
P.O. Box 2212, Stn. R.
Kelowna, B.C. Canada

Narrow Way Ministries
P.O. Box 367
Holbrook, NY 11741

CARIS
P.O. Box 1783
Santa Ana, Ca. 92702

Witness, Inc.
P.O. Box 597
Clayton, Ca. 94517

April 7, 1981

Congregation Servant
Jehovah's Witnesses

Dear Sir:

The enclosed letter has been sent to your headquarters in Brooklyn. From my research and experience it is likely that they will warn you not to pay any attention to this material, but they would not send you a copy nor discuss the points of my letter with you. So you could not ever know for sure what the letter contained.

Therefore, I am sending an exact copy to you. Whatever your reaction may be, at least you can know what was really said.

It is my hope and prayer that you will deal fairly with this material. If you don't read it you can't judge it.

Very sincerely yours,
Gordon E. Duggar

GED/ab
Enclosures

April 7, 1981

Watchtower
117 Adams Street
Brooklyn, New York 11201

Gentlemen:

About three years ago I wrote you after a relative had given us a copy of one of your publications. Because I have been associated with your movement for thirty years out of your 100 years, I recognized a change in your doctrinal position. The disturbing thing to me was the way you published the change. This has led me to a very extensive review of your literature and activities and doctrines since the beginning of the Watchtower.

I find it absolutely mind-boggling that you are so able to completely capture the minds of so many of your followers. You—who claim to know the TRUTH—*the only TRUTH*—take incredible liberties with truth. I have before me a long list of examples wherein your organization has deceptively, dishonestly, and distortedly misrepresented the truth. I also find it difficult to believe that at least some of your headquarters staff don't stand up in rage when they witness what all KNOW to be deliberate misrepresentations. Are there sincere, repentant Christians there? As I have seen in your local congregations, is it because they know better than to raise a voice to question? What would happen to them? I know, and you know what would happen to them! Just which ones of the Brooklyn 'remnant' have authority from Jehovah to decide on procedure to slant or deceptively revise? Who authorizes such deception?

Your "AID" book defines a lie as not telling the truth to someone who is entitled to know the truth. Is there a degree, or degrees, of truth? Can we pick out those who are NOT entitled to know the truth? Is deception congruous with truth? God's truth? *God's ONLY TRUTH?*

There is no way for you to say that the following example does not clearly demonstrate your deliberate, deceptive, gloss-over of a failed prophesy. *Yearbook,* 1975, Page 146. On the expected return of the "ancient worthies" in 1925.

"1925 was a sad year for many brothers . . . Instead of its being considered a 'probability,' they read into it that it was a 'certainty', . . .

Now just why did the brothers consider a "certainty" rather than a probability? You know why they did and I know why they did. Your leader, your prophet (by your own description), the "faithful and discreet slave" said, in your own publications:

The year was 1920. Your publication said:
". . . the second world, legally ended in 1914, and since that time has been and is passing away; that the new order of things is coming in to take its place; that within a definite period of time the old order will be completely eradicated and the new order in full sway; and that these things shall take place within the time of the present generation and that therefore there are millions of people now living on earth who will see them take place, to whom everlasting life will be offered and who . . . will never die."
And, in the same book under the heading 'Positive Promise':
". . . and that 1925 shall mark the resurrection of the faithful worthies of old. . . ."
The bottom of it all is to realize that the Organization has the audacity to blame error on the 'brothers'; the followers; the meek lambs who simply accept the 'meat in due season'; who truly accept what you say as being straight from Jehovah.

There is a further problem with this same subject. How do they know when to believe what you print? In another book, in 1932, the same 'prophet' the same 'faithful slave' published this 'prophecy':
"This prophecy, therefore, shows that Christ the King will make those faithful men the princes or visible rulers in all the earth. That means that soon you may expect to see Abraham, Enoch, Moses, David and all of these other faithful men back on earth."
Honestly now, can we say that the prophecy failed because the members misunderstood or jumped to wrong conclusions? Is this honest? Is this a credible act for the organization of God? Is this what you are into when one is 'in the Truth'? Are you pleased with yourselves when you *know* what you have done to your followers? Does Jehovah approve of deception?

The cynical attitude toward non-witnesses that you have developed in your followers (don't say it isn't so and don't deny responsibility) makes these people distrust all others—doctors, lawyers, even carpenters. From personal experience I know this is true. Yet, unless some of the 'worldly' were not Witnesses there would be no doctors or lawyers. You have told your followers there wasn't time for college, yet in 100 years you would have had time to raise some up had it not been for your Armageddon complex. I scold you severely for propagating this attitude toward your membership. All significant cultures, except you, have encouraged education. This is of God.

I hope you take this seriously. It is not written by an ex-Witness who is mad at the Society. Fact is, for years I held the Society in respect and esteem. At one time I felt this might be just what you claim. If so, it should stand the test. Well, the people who make up your membership do stand the test. They are people, just people like the rest of us. But your doctrines and orders from headquarters mislead and stumble them. Some will admit it, some won't. But, devout hell-bent for leather JW's all *fear* the Society. They fear your wrath upon them. I have been able to personally observe this in several instances. You tell your people that Jehovah is so much love He would not provide punishment for sin, yet you also tell them this same Jehovah forbids a life-saving blood transfusion. You don't tell your members straight out that the 'slave' only discovered this fact in 1945 (6000 years after Leviticus). Do you think there is any hope for those Witnesses who had a transfusion in 1920, or 1930, or 1940? How about the fact that Hebrew law was written thousands of years ago (even the book of ACTS was written 2000 years ago) but transfusions were not done until the early 1900's. Was Jehovah warning 6000 years in advance against an act unknown to the Hebrews? And if so, why did Witnesses before 1945 not recognize the violations by His chosen ones, some of whom were 'anointed'? In a 1978 *Watchtower* you admonished that followers can follow their consciences in regard to receiving a small amount of blood in an injection. What kind of law is this?

The cynical attitude is also seen in situations of personal importance to Witnesses. Very recently, a patient was assured that, at risk of her life itself, she would receive no blood. She felt very much a martyr. When the patient was longer than expected in the operating room, her Witness relative expressed the feeling that the delay was due to the fact, she feared, that they were trying to give the patient blood!

You stand warned. The lives of these people are in your hands. At one time you disallowed vaccinations (and your children were scratched in pretense). I hope none died because of your 'interpretation' which has now changed.

Just suppose you later change your mind about transfusions (get more light). Do you feel any responsibility? Jehovah God will hold you who produce and print these deceptions fully accountable.

The strong evidence of a falling away from your organization is testimony to the problems you face. The marked reduction in magazines and hours spent by publishers coupled with increased efforts by the Society to keep 'em working suggest the Society may be losing its grip on the people. I pray you are. But, more I pray a move of repentance among Watchtower leadership. Your dictators are gone. Someone there must take the lead.

The person who reads this letter has responsibility to deal with the matter. If you present it to others they also have responsibility. You are responsible before Jehovah for the two million innocent followers. You can refuse, you can justify, but you cannot deny the deception. No organization truly of God is built on deceit. May the cloud of responsibility hang heavy over you. It is not necessary to reply but a reply is welcome. Don't send any booklets.

Sincerely,
Gordon E. Duggar

GED/ab

In a previous Questions from Readers in a recent *Watchtower* magazine, someone has realized that a statement is made in the "Commentary on the Letter of James," page 47, which is not in keeping with Watchtower interpretation of doctrine. In the commentary on James 1:27 ("The form of worship that is clean and undefiled from the standpoint of our God and Father is this."), the verse is explained correctly: "Besides being the God of Christians, Jehovah is also their Father, for he has begotten them by means of his spirit to be his sons." This is undoubtedly good news to the reader who asks if this means that all dedicated and baptized Christians have been begotten by God's Spirit so as to be his sons. Of course, this is clearly what the commentary says and also clearly what the Scripture says.

But look at the answer. The answer given is no, that this meaning should not be given to the passage, because if so it would nullify other Watchtower interpretations of Scripture.

Think on that statement. The next phase of the answer is unbelievable. The explanation is given that the author of the commentary *took for granted* that the reader, because of earlier comments about the first verse, would appreciate that all Christians were not included. To avoid ambiguity you say that the word "anointed" could be inserted before the word "Christians." This would also avoid something else—the true meaning of the verse.

Oh foolish Watchtower! You know this verse does not suggest nor infer "anointed" or any other special adjective. The text is (James 1:27 NW): "The form of worship that is clean and undefiled from the standpoint of our God and Father is this:" (some texts read "God the Father"). The rest of this verse is directed toward the care of orphans and widows. Is this the responsibility of the "anointed"? In text or context the meaning of this straightforward verse is not clouded nor filled with any Scriptural innuendo.

The Watchtower explains that James 1:1 refers to the "144,000." Do you agree? Then notice this:

In verse 5, some lack wisdom. Some are doubters (verse 6). Some are two-faced (verse 8). Verses 9 and 10 refer to poor and rich. Verse 21 warns to put away any filthiness. Verses 22 warns to be not just hearers (to whom do you apply this?). Chapter 2:1 warns against favoritism. 2:6 says they have (the anointed?) dishonored the poor. Chapter 3 warns about danger of the tongue. Chapter 4 warns about worldliness and pride. Verses 2-6 say that they kill, fight, war, commit adultery. (Are we still talking about the anointed?) Chapter Five warns the rich (you have lived in luxury on earth) and warns against unchristian conduct. 5:12 warns to stop swearing, and verse 16 admonishes to openly confess sin. Do you still insist the above applies (only) to the anointed? Is this your view of anointed? Then what's so special about being anointed? One translation for James 1:1 is "Greetings to all God's people scattered over the whole world." When your followers begin to realize some of these things, your organization will be in trouble.

But besides all this, there is no way to interpret James 1:27

any other way than you have done in your Commentary on the Letter of James. In your KIT there are no words other than "our God and Father." That's all the text says. That's all the Greek says. In your "Questions from Readers" you have deceived them again. Tell me now. Are the ones who wrote this commentary the same ones you reprimanded and disfellowshipped recently for "apostasy," because they felt all Christians are born-again children of God? Are these the same people? How could you insert "anointed" when it is not there in text nor context? Because your doctrine demands it, not because it is truth. SHAME ON YOU!

ADDITIONAL REFERENCES TO "God the Father." Check the text and context in each case. New World Translation.

Isaiah	9: 6	(and Jesus will be called) Eternal Father
	63:16	(You, or Jehovah, are our Father)
Jer.	31: 9	I have become to Israel (the nation) a Father
Mal.	2:10	Is it not one Father that all of us have? Is it not one God that has created us?
Matt.	5:16	Give glory to your Father who is in heaven (Jesus speaking to the crowds and to the disciples, some of whom you teach will have an earthly reward.)
	6: 8	God your Father
	6: 9	Our Father in the heavens
	28:19	Baptize them in the name of the Father
Luke	6:36	Your Father is merciful
	12:32	Your Father
John	5:23	honor the Son just as they honor the Father
	14: 6	No one comes to the Father except through me
Romans	8:15-16	by which Spirit we cry out Abba, Father . . . we are all God's children. (To the Romans "to all those who are in Rome as God's beloved ones, called to be holy ones" (1:7)

Gal.   4: 6, 7 Abba, Father. So, then, you are no longer a
                 slave but a son (to the *congregations* of
                 Galatia 1:2)
1 John   3: 1   so that we should be called the children of
                 God, and such we are.

There is no Scripture to indicate that Jehovah, in a "unique
way" (your words) is Father to the anointed on the one hand,
and also, in some other way, is Father to those with an earthly
destiny.

In Matthew, Chapter 6, Jesus addressed the *multitude* (not
the anointed). In eighteen verses Jesus referred to 'Your Father'
ten times. In teaching them to pray Jesus said: "You must pray,
then, this way: Our Father in the heavens." This Scripture is
just as clear, in text and in context, as is James 1:27. So, your
commentary was correct. James was addressing the *Christians*.
Period.

There is further evidence in this commentary which indicates
more trouble for you, which indicates these authors leaned toward
further deviation from Watchtower doctrine (and closer to real
Scriptural truth). As a matter of fact, the introduction beginning
on page five provides suggestions as to whom the Letter of
James applied. The very first statement reads "The Letter of
James is a call to practical Christianity on the part of *all claiming
to have faith in Christ* (emphasis added)". And in the second
paragraph: "His letter is referred to as a "general epistle" because
it was not addressed to any specific congregation or person, as
were most of the letters of the Apostle Paul and Second and
Third John."

There is more trouble for you: Page six: "We cannot
properly devise a formula or build a structure through which we
can work out our salvation. The faith must be there first. As
James deeply emphasized, good works will come spontaneously
from the heart . . ." If this be true, and it is, why do you have
to put so much "heat" on your followers to go out to place your
magazines? Even you could not call this "spontaneous" if you
review your records, especially right now.

Page twenty-six (26), explaining James 1:12 "because on becoming approved he will receive the crown of life." The commentary explains the verse: "By remaining an approved servant of Jehovah, the spirit-begotten Christian is sure to receive the 'crown' of life." *This does not mean that he earns the right to life by his* ENDURANCE OF TRIALS, but he is honored as with a "crown" by the gift of heavenly life. Life cannot be earned by imperfect humans *but is the free gift through faith in Jesus Christ.* The enduring *Christian has proved that he has that faith.* Say, now, "Christendom" has taught this from the beginning. (Witnesses, someone there at Headquarters is sending you a signal.) Did you leave out a word again? The questions for this verse on page 53 ask: What is the promise to the Christian (you need to add 'anointed' again) who endures to the end through trials? Does the faithfully enduring Christian (oops) earn life or receive it as wages or a reward?" Verse 12 had said, "Happy is the man that keeps on enduring trials" (Oh, dear! the Bible forgot and also left out "anointed").

Page 84: "However, James is not writing to the Jews as a nation. He is addressing the scattered Christians, from both Jewish and Gentile stock." This may make you cringe. On page 13 of the commentary, the 12,000 of each tribe is said to be a symbolic number (Rev. 7:4-8). If 12,000 is symbolic, would not 144,000 also be symbolic? How much proof do we need? AND from your own writings!

I have been told by a knowledgeable Christian that God will not deny the millions of sincere, devoted people who are mistakenly seeking Jehovah through the Watchtower. These will be, apparently are now, given opportunity to see real truth—even to compare it with Watchtower error. With this in mind, perhaps Jehovah is at this time working through the leaders there, either to bring repentance or exposure. God could use you—remember SAUL/PAUL? AMEN!

References

WATCHTOWER LITERATURE

1. *The Divine Plan of the Ages.* C. T. Russell, 1886.
2. *The Divine Plan of the Ages.* C. T. Russell, 1927.
3. *Prophecy.* J. F. Rutherford, 1929.
4. *Creation.* J. F. Rutherford, 1927.
5. *Preparation.* J. F. Rutherford, 1933.
6. *Light,* book II. J. F. Rutherford, 1930.
7. *Preservation.* J. F. Rutherford, 1932.
8. *Riches.* J. F. Rutherford, 1936.
9. *Life.* J. F. Rutherford, 1929.
10. *Government. J. F. Rutherford,* 1928.
11. *Children.* J. F. Rutherford, 1941.
12. *Millions Now Living Will Never Die.* J. F. Rutherford, 1920.
13. *The New World.* 1942.
14. *The Truth Shall Make You Free.* 1943.
15. *The Kingdom Is At Hand.* 1944.
16. *Qualified To Be Ministers.* 1955.
17. *New Heavens and a New Earth.* 1953.
18. *What Has Religion Done for Mankind?* 1951.
19. *Your Word Is a Lamp to My Feet.* 1967.
20. *God's Kingdom of a Thousand Years Has Approached.* 1973.
21. *Make Sure of All Things.* 1965.
22. *The Truth That Leads to Eternal Life.* 1968.
23. *Organization for Kingdom—Preaching and Disciple-Making.* 1972.
24. *Our Incoming World Government—God's Kingdom.* 1977.
25. *1977 Yearbook of Jehovah's Witnesses.*
26. *The Watchtower,* bound volume, 1968, 1973, 1974.
27. *Aid to Bible Understanding.* 1969.
28. *What You Need.* J. F. Rutherford, 1932 (especially page 8).
29. *New World Translation of the Holy Scriptures.* 1970.
30. *The Kingdom Interlinear Translation of the Greek Scripture.* 1969.

122

31. *Comprehensive Concordance of the New World Translation.* 1973.
32. *1974 Yearbook of Jehovah's Witnesses.*
33. *Let God Be True.* 1952.
34. *God's Eternal Purpose Now Triumphing.* 1974.
35. *Let Your Name Be Sanctified.* 1961.
36. *Man's Salvation Out of World Distress at Hand.* 1975.
37. *Emphatic Diaglott,* Benjamin Wilson, 1942.
38. *Is the Bible Really the Word of God?* 1969.
39. *Things in Which It Is Impossible for God To Lie.* 1965.
40. *Listening to the Great Teacher.* 1971.
41. *Babylon the Great Has Fallen!* 1963.
42. *The Nations Shall Know That I Am Jehovah—How?* 1971.
43. *Holy Spirit. The Force Behind the Coming New Order.* 1976.
44. *Then Is Finished the Mystery of God.* 1969.
45. *True Peace and Security.* 1973.
46. *My Book of Bible Stories.* 1978.
47. *Paradise Restored to Mankind—by Theocracy.* 1972.
48. *Jehovah's Witnesses in the Twentieth Century.* 1978.
49. Numerous individual issues of the *Watchtower* magazine.

BOOKS SYMPATHETIC TO THE WITNESSES

1. *Faith on the March.* A. H. MacMillan (New Jersey: Prentice-Hall, 1957). An autobiography by a Witness officer.
2. *Jehovah's Witnesses: The New World Society.* Marley Cole (New York: Vantage Press, 1955).
3. *Jehovah's Witnesses in the Divine Purpose* (New York: Watchtower Bible and Tract Society, 1959). Their own version of the history of the Witnesses (as of 1959).

DOCTRINAL INVESTIGATIONS OF THE JEHOVAH'S WITNESSES

1. *Jehovah of the Watchtower.* Martin and Klann (Michigan: Zondervan Publications, 1959). An exhaustive investigation.
2. *Jehovah's Witnesses.* Walter R. Martin (Minnesota: Bethany Fellowship, Inc., 1957).
3. *Jehovah's Witnesses Errors Exposed.* William J. Schnell (Michigan: Baker Book House, 1959).
4. *The Bible, the Christian, and Jehovah's Witnesses.* Gordon R. Lewis (New Jersey: Presbyterian and Reformed Publishing Co., 1976).
5. *The Scholastic Dishonesty of the Watchtower.* Michael Van

Buskirk (C.A.R.I.S., P.O. Box 1783, Santa Ana, Ca. 92702, 1976). Contains undeniable proof of journalistic dishonesty of the Watchtower Society.

6. *Cults and the Occult in the Age of Aquarius.* Edmond C. Gruss (Michigan: Baker Book House, 1974).

7. *Jehovah's Witnesses.* Anthony A. Hoekema (Michigan: William B. Eerdmans Publishing Co., 1972).

8. *Jehovah's Witnesses and Prophetic Speculation.* Edmond C. Gruss (New Jersey: Presbyterian and Reformed Publishing Co., 1976). An examination and refutation of the Witnesses' position on the Second Coming of Christ. Armageddon and other doctrines, by an ex-Jehovah's Witness.

BOOKS BY EX-WITNESSES: TESTIMONIES

1. *Thirty Years a Watchtower Slave.* William J. Schnell (Michigan: Baker Book House, 1971).

2. *We Left Jehovah's Witnesses.* Edmond C. Gruss (New Jersey: Presbyterian and Reformed Publishing Co., 1977).

3. *Kicked Out of the Watchtower.* Valerie Tomsett (England: Cox and Wynn, Ltd., 1974).

5. *The Watchtower Doors Begin to Open.* Erich and Jean Grieshaben (P.O. Box 4295. Santa Clara, California 95050). 1975.

6. *The Inside Story of Jehovah's Witnesses.* W. C. Stevenson. (Pennsylvania: Hart Publishing Co., 1967).

7. *Apostles of Denial.* Edmond C. Gruss (Pennsylvania: Presbyterian and Reformed Publishing Co., 1970).

8. *Why I Left Jehovah's Witnesses.* Ted Dencher (Pennsylvania: Christian Literature Crusade, 1966).

TAPES*

1. "Out of the Watchtower." Tapes by William Cetnar.

2. Testimony of various ex-witnesses. Watchman Fellowship, P.O. Box 7681, Columbus, Georgia 31908.

3. "The Watchtower Forum." An extensive examination of the Witnesses.

4. "We Walked Away from the Watchtower—Testimonies of Ex-Witnesses."

*Tapes 3-7 available from C.A.R.I.S., P.O. Box 1783, Santa Ana, CA 92702.

5. "Jehovah's Witnesses Debate Tapes." A debate held in a church with Witnesses.

6. "Dr. Julius Mantey on Jehovah's Witnesses and the Deity of Christ."

7. "Scholastic Dishonesty of the Watchtower." Michael Van Buskirk.

OTHER REFERENCE WORKS

1. *The Tabernacle: Camping with God.* Stephen Olford (New Jersey: Loizeaux Brothers Publishers, 1971).

2. *The Names of God.* Andrew Jukes (Michigan: Kregel Publications, first ed., 1888; second American printing, 1978).